Jan Paulsen

Where We Are Going?

Pacific Press® Publishing Associ:
Nampa, Idaho
Oshawa, Ontario, Canada
www.pacificpress.com

D1615355

Also by Jan Paulsen

Let Your Life So Shine

When the Spirit Descends

In Appreciation

God and His people are indescribably important to me. My love for them and commitment to them know no measure. They are my life. I thank God and the church for the opportunities to serve that I have been given. At times, it has gone well; but, at times, it has also been flawed. Nevertheless and in all, thank you.

I am grateful also to colleagues in leadership who have made it possible for me to function and to grow. They were patient and very supportive—with an understanding of human limitations. I say thank you to them.

To Kari, my wife and special companion in more than fifty years of ministry, and to our children—well, let me not try to put my thoughts into words. Just thank you for what you have been to me.

My very able and gifted assistant Bettina Krause has been an important partner in the production of this book, not only in editorial work but also in critiquing my points and strengthening and making clear what I am trying to say. Thank you, Bettina.

And thank you to Pacific Press for being the instrument to bring this book to the public.

Jan Paulsen
April 2011

Cover design by Gerald Lee Monks
Cover design resources from the General Conference Office
Inside design by Aaron Troia

The author assumes full responsibility for the accuracy of all facts and quotations as cited in this book.

Unless otherwise marked, Bible texts quoted in this book are from THE HOLY BIBLE, NEW INTERNATIONAL VERSION®, NIV®. Copyright © 1973, 1978, 1984, 2011 by Biblica, Inc.™ Used by permission. All rights reserved worldwide.

Bible texts marked KJV are from the King James Version.

Bible texts marked ISV are taken from The Holy Bible: International Standard Version. Copyright © 1994-2008 by the ISV Foundation. ALL RIGHTS RESERVED INTERNATIONALLY.

Scripture quotations marked *The Message* are from *The Message*. Copyright © by Eugene H. Peterson, 1993, 1994, 1995, 1996, 2000, 2001, 2002. Used by permisson of NavPress Publishing Group.

You can obtain additional copies of this book by calling toll-free 1-800-765-6955 or by visiting http://www.adventistbookcenter.com.

Library of Congress Cataloging-in-Publication Data

Paulsen, Jan.
    Where are you going? : we have nothing to fear for the future, except we shall forget the way the Lord has led us, and his teaching in our past history / Jan Paulsen.
        p. cm.
    ISBN 13: 978-0-8163-2509-2 (pbk.)
    ISBN 10: 0-8163-2509-X (pbk.)
    1. Christian leadership—Seventh-day Adventists. 2. Seventh-day Adventists—Doctrines. I. Title.
    BV652.1.P389 2011
    253—dc23
                                                                2011021009

11 12 13 14 15 • 5 4 3 2 1

Contents

Preface... 7

Introduction 9

Chapter 1   My Journey.. 15

Chapter 2   What Drives Us?... 28

Chapter 3   Bring Them in From the Cold.................... 38

Chapter 4   "People From Elsewhere".......................... 47

Chapter 5   The Church and "Other People" 54

Chapter 6   The Church and Other Churches 62

Chapter 7   The President and His Associates.............. 73

Chapter 8   Choosing a Leader Isn't Easy!................... 82

Chapter 9   Unity—Being *One* Body.......................... 91

Chapter 10 A Place Where We Can Feel at Home.......101

Chapter 11 Living in Tension.....................................109

Chapter 12 Reflections on What Lies Ahead 118

Preface

Shortly after I'd been elected president of the one of the Seventh-day Adventist Church's world divisions, a woman from my home country, Norway, shared with me her delight at what had happened. Her delight was not so much that I had been elected but that someone had been elected who was *not* from one of the leadership dynasties of the church. She herself had married into a family in which church leadership was something of a family business, and from her privileged position on the inside, she had seen and reflected on some of the goings-on. I sensed that she was none too impressed. Yet I had come from nowhere and had been elected to senior leadership positions of the Adventist Church in more than twenty countries. "How absolutely wonderful!" she said.

As the years have passed, I've reflected on her reaction, and I've become firmly convinced that no nationality, no race, and no individual has exclusive rights to any leadership position within the church. The church's offices can't be passed along as an inheritance. They're not entitlements. God has—and His people must also have—total freedom in the choice of leaders. God guided in the choosing of David of old, who came from nowhere. He will lead His people to make unexpected choices any time He wants to.

That's how I became a leader. God surprised me—as He often does.

Jan Paulsen

Introduction

As a leader, the apostle Peter was a study in contradictions. He was brave and loyal, yet also given to bouts of cowardice. He could be overconfident and hasty of tongue, yet his leadership within the early Christian church exemplified rock-solid steadiness of purpose. He began as someone who possessed in almost equal measure both great leadership potential and great potential for messing up. Yet under Christ's tutelage and the leading of the Spirit, we see Peter mature into an extraordinary leader of God's people. In his complex mix of strength and weakness, good intentions and human inconsistencies, Peter was much like many of us.

I like the old story that's told about the later years of Peter's ministry—and it's just a story, no doubt utterly apocryphal. According to the ancient tale, Christians in the pagan city of Rome are once again being targeted for persecution, and Peter is caught up in the panic that races through the Christian community, so he decides to flee.

On his way out of Rome, Peter meets the crucified and resurrected Lord, who is heading into the city. Startled, Peter asks Jesus, *"Quo vadis, Domine?"*—"Where are you going, Lord?" The Master replies, "I'm on my way into Rome to be crucified afresh."

According to the story, this stops Peter. He takes the Lord's comment to mean that the Lord will suffer death again in the life of His disciple Peter. So Peter turns around and goes back to Rome, where he later suffers martyrdom.

Yes, it's just a story, but it invites a provocative thought. If those entrusted by the Lord with leadership assignments—whether in the local church or elsewhere—were to walk away from their responsibilities, the Master might confront them and ask, "Is this the direction you want to go?" Or He might just look to someone else to carry forward His mission of sharing salvation with lost humanity. The Lord Himself is always the One who sets the direction and defines the agenda for His people, and we must commit ourselves to be obedient to His will.

As Seventh-day Adventist leaders, our choice of direction is critical. How did we make that choice? Did we hear His voice? Do we know where we are going and why? Are we focused on the task at hand, which is mission? Or have various distractions—church politics, personal ambition, or just plain leadership burnout—turned our steps away from the priorities to which Christ is calling us?

The market today is flooded with books on leadership, both secular and religious. It's difficult to imagine any area that's not covered by how-to leadership material. So, what is the point of this book? Does it take readers where others do not? You'll be the judge of that, but what I've written here isn't advice I've gathered by research in books. Rather, it's the perspective I've developed through a lifetime of personal experience.

This book is not a continuous narrative. Instead, it's a series of reflections on issues that are important to the life of our church, issues that leadership must address. They're issues I've encountered on my journey—some of them being matters I wish I could have resolved more effectively than I did.

The Adventist Church has become a very complex global community of some twenty-five to thirty million people, both young and old. It's established in more than two hundred countries. It operates a massive range of services. Its "business" is conducted in almost all imaginable languages. And it spans a multitude of different cultures and people groups. How is this sprawling, diverse worldwide community organized and managed? Is it hierarchical—does it have elements of the Vatican model? What role does local leadership play? Are local leaders autonomous decision makers or do they owe accountability to the larger body? Are Adventist institutions—schools, hospitals, and publishing houses—loosely related entities, charting their own courses, defining their own values, and "answering only to God," the oft-used escape clause people use to avoid accountability?

Early in our church's history, we decided that we would stay together as one global organization. We would share biblically based spiritual and moral values, which would become identifying marks of our community around the world. I believe that to this end, God led us to set in place a system of governance that allows for worldwide consultation and input.

What does this mean in practice? It means that our identity is owned by the global church. Adventism is not North American, European, African, Asian, Australian, or Latin American. It is *global,* and it is just *Adventist*—with no geographic qualifiers. There is no such thing as a national Adventist Church with its own value system or identity.

This doesn't mean we're culturally homogenous. As General Conference president, I saw an incredible range of ways people can "be Adventist" within their own culture. Our core values remain unchanged, but our culture lends a special flavor to our faith. Members in the United States and Canada will worship in different ways than do members in Kenya, Brazil, Korea, Germany, and Jamaica. But I believe these differences in how we live, look, eat, speak, and worship our Lord are mainly cosmetic. When we dig a little below the surface, we find a fundamental resemblance, something I've experienced time and time again.

Through the decades, we've stayed together as a church and weathered difficult times in large part because we talk to each other. Church leaders from around the world meet at least once a year at what is known as Annual Council. Although it's usually described as a business meeting, in essence, Annual Council is the time each year when world church leaders reaffirm to each other and to God that we will work together as one people, with one faith and one mission.

At Annual Council, church leaders consult, seek consensus, and draft policies and guidelines for the whole church. We debate the global mission agenda of the church. We set directions and spell out priorities. We talk about how we will share resources, financial and otherwise. Do we always agree? Of course not. But these meetings are marked by a pervasive sense of global ownership, a sense that local and national interests must give way before the needs of the larger community.

In the first decade of this century, church leaders meeting at Annual Councils took up issues of tremendous importance. We considered Fundamental Belief number 6—"Creation"—and comprehensively rejected any notion of evolution as an explanation of origins. We strongly affirmed the historic position of the church that Creation, as introduced in Genesis 1 and 2, took place in one week of seven literal days, celebrated by the Sabbath, which marked the end of the Creation week.

Annual Councils have also looked at church structure and introduced more flexibility for forming "Unions of Churches," thus eliminating a layer of administration where this would allow us to use resources more efficiently and better position us for mission.

Leaders have also considered the role of women in ministry—an issue that we will explore at greater length later in this book. The church has never taken the view that biblical teachings exclude the possibility of women being ordained to ministry on an equal footing with men. But global leadership has felt that local readiness and perceptions—heavily influenced by culture—have thus far kept us from moving forward on this as a global community. For some members, women having a role in ministry is not a problem, but for others it is. So there's no doubt this discussion still has some distance to go; it's not going away.

Areas of significant disagreement, such as the precise role of women in ministry, demonstrate clearly that in our multicultural church we have to do better at listening to each other with understanding. It's particularly important that those of us who are leaders in the church be able to listen to someone who thinks differently—who perhaps vehemently disagrees with us!—and yet not feel threatened.

Difficult issues raise the question as to whether global leaders should ever walk away from consensus. Are we ever entitled to say, "Well, this may not work for you, but it works well for my church in my part of the world. This is what *we* must do to be obedient to God where we live"?

I believe that global unity is a nonnegotiable value for the Adventist

Introduction

Church, and thus you cannot impose on a global community something that major segments of that community find unacceptable. Witness the recent experience of other denominations that have fragmented over the question of the ordination of gay clergy or their consecration to senior church offices.

Preserving unity, even in the presence of disagreement, is a leadership issue, for if leaders will not face this task, who will?

I've talked with some leaders who would prefer to deal with differences in the global community by the "easier" method of turning a blind eye to local aberrations. But in the long run, that approach is untenable. It may be difficult to wrestle with diversity and to search for up-front ways to accommodate it, but doing so is the only sustainable way to deal with differences without breaching the unity of the global church.

Thinking locally as well as globally is not easy, and finding enough leaders who can do so is especially challenging in a dynamic, growing organization such as ours. With some seven thousand schools and universities, six hundred hospitals and clinics, and a force of some thirty thousand ministers, there is a constant demand for leadership personnel to keep it all going. It's fair to ask, "How do we train an adequate pool of high-quality leaders who can meet the needs of the church locally, but who also have allegiance to the wider, international body?"

The process of electing leadership plays a very important role in our church—from the local congregation to the General Conference. While there may be slight differences in forms or procedures, the essential ingredient in all of our electoral processes is delegated authority. Human authority within our church doesn't follow a hierarchical model, flowing downward, from top to bottom. Instead, the power of choosing the church's leaders lies in the hands of individuals who've been entrusted to represent their fellow church members in the decision-making process. Beyond the mere mechanics of our electoral system, though, we also acknowledge a more important force at work: the Holy Spirit responding to our invitation for Him to prompt and guide us in what would otherwise surely be a difficult and risky enterprise.

Some may wonder whether ulterior factors that smell of political influence or secret deals tarnish an otherwise beautiful concept. Is it possible that God, who is present to guide the church in these elections, is sometimes left with a less-than-best choice simply because we compromised our values? We'll explore such questions in a later chapter, but I strongly believe that the presence of the Holy Spirit, in response to prayer, *will* guide the process if we allow Him to work and if we keep our hearts pure.

So, against the backdrop of all these challenges, I ask again the question, As Adventist Church leaders—local elders and pastors; school and hospital administrators; conference, union, and General Conference administrators—*quo vadis?* Where are we going? Are we walking toward or away from the task Christ has given us? Can we really know what He expects of us?

The coming pages record some perspectives on leadership that I've developed through the years, as well as some often hard-learned lessons that I've absorbed along the way. Each of you will recognize that the experience of leadership can bring a tremendous sense of purpose, joy, and fulfillment, while at the same time yielding up ample servings of pain, vulnerability, and seemingly impossible situations. Yet for each of us there is one constant: no matter what circumstances we face, we can be sure of the abiding presence of our Lord. For this is His church, and we are His servants.

Chapter 1

My Journey

As leaders, we can't escape our personal histories. The decisions we make today—our unconscious "default" positions, our response to challenging people or issues, the way we define our leadership role—are all shaped profoundly by the path we've traveled and our experiences along the way.

My journey began two hundred miles north of the Arctic Circle in Norway during the depression of the 1930s. The Adventist Church went through a strong growth and revival in north Norway during those years, and my parents were a part of that. They were baptized, joined the church, and created for their children a warm and faith-affirming Adventist home. I learned early in my life to value the spiritual nurture of Ellen White's writings. As a child, I felt we were special. We were different, but we differed in a positive way.

At that time, being poor was considered normal. One day, I said to my father, "We're not really poor—we eat every day!" He just looked at me. He was a cobbler, and feeding his family of three children was just about all he could do.

My father had set up a small shop to fix shoes because as a Seventh-day Adventist in north Norway at that time it wasn't easy to find employment. Those were the days of forty-eight-hour work weeks, and it was the rare employer who would look twice at someone who wouldn't work on the Sabbath. The situation was complicated even more by the Arctic Circle Sabbath, which in the dead of winter began at midday on Friday. To employ someone who would be gone for much of each Friday for a good part of the year—well, it was usually too difficult.

We were poor, but there was a sense of honor in it. In our community, we empathized with each other, we helped out when we could, and we didn't take advantage of anyone. For me, it was good to learn early in life to live with little.

The Second World War came to Norway when I was five years old. The occupying German soldiers had set up a prisoner-of-war camp in Beisfjord, outside Narvik, to hold some Serbian prisoners. I remember looking at them through the barbed-wire fencing and asking my mother, "What have they done?"

She said, "Nothing. They are just from another country."

That was my first exposure to ethnic cleansing and the strong, irrational feelings that sometimes flow from cultural or national allegiances. Even then, I just knew it didn't make sense and it was wrong.

Lesson for a five-year-old boy: No one should have to suffer because of where they come from or what they look like.

During the next five years, I lived with my family in an old school building that we shared with three hundred German soldiers. We lived in the caretaker's flat, and the classrooms were the soldiers' bedrooms. My childhood memories from those years are mostly good. The soldiers meant us no harm. They were busy training for arctic warfare, and we just got on with our lives. War or peace, shoes wear out and need repair, and my father kept his repair shop going.

One night, toward the end of the war, I heard the sound of someone crying coming from one of the rooms occupied by the German soldiers. I asked my mother, "Why are they crying?"

She said, "Well, they're just boys. They miss their mommies and daddies, and they just want to go home." Some of those soldiers were just boys of fourteen or fifteen years of age.

Lesson for a ten-year-old boy: Whether you are one of the perpetrators or one of the victims, war hands out suffering indiscriminately.

My Journey

One summer, toward the end of the war, a man from the hills—he belonged to a people group we called Lapps—came to my father's shoe-repair shop and asked to borrow one of his sons for a couple of months. The Lapp needed someone to help look after his herds of sheep and goats in the hills where he lived. "I'll look after your boy well, feed him well, and give him some new winter clothes as payment," he promised.

Although my brother was a bit older than me, I was slightly bigger, so it was decided that I could go with the Lapp. It meant that I'd spend the summer some fifteen miles away from my family, which was a vast distance when the only transportation options were bicycle, horse, or one's own two legs.

For me, that summer was a traumatic experience. The Lapp had promised my father I wouldn't have to work on the Sabbath, but I quickly lost track of the days, and it soon became apparent that my employer was determined to get the most out of me. I'd better not describe the food he gave me! It was nothing like my simple menu from home. I missed my family terribly, but when I cried, he laughed at me. I was convinced I'd been forgotten, nobody loved me, and I would never see my family again.

In the middle of one of my nights there, the Lapp woke me and said two goats were missing. "Go back into the hills and find them," he told me.

"But it's the middle of the night, and it's raining hard," I protested, to no avail. I remember feeling utterly rejected and abandoned. The water that ran down my face tasted salty—it was a mix of rain and tears. Then something warm touched my hand, and I looked down and saw my dog, my constant companion. He sensed my aloneness, and he reminded me that he was there. Somehow, together, we found the goats and brought them back down from the hills, and I was able to go back to sleep again.

When my father came at the end of the summer to take me home, the "pay" for my work was a pair of hand-knitted mittens. In the years that followed, my father told me many times, "I should never have let you go." But it happened, and I learned a lesson that has stayed with me.

Lesson for a boy who felt abandoned: The Holy Spirit is a constant Companion,

even in difficult moments. He is there in the midst of success and of failure—
and in everything in between.

When there's little love

My mother's parents belonged to an austere, pietistic branch of the Lutheran Church known locally as *Laestadianer*—followers of a Lutheran revivalist named Laestadius. My grandfather's austerity expressed itself in a joyless and severe Christianity. No flowerpots on the windowsills and no neckties. If you laughed and were happy, you were made to feel guilty. I can still hear him saying to me as a boy, "Don't whistle. If you whistle, you call on the devil."

He believed my father had led his daughter into an "apostate sect," and he maintained a hostile attitude toward our family. My grandparents were among the lucky ones during those hand-to-mouth years because they had a small farm and could grow their own vegetables and keep a few cows. To punish us for being Adventists, my grandfather refused to sell us potatoes. But we went elsewhere, and we survived.

Lessons for a hungry child:
- *Being a follower of Christ shouldn't be a joyless experience.*
- *No one has the right to judge and condemn others on account of what they believe.*
- *Don't deny potatoes to those who have none. And especially, don't be cruel to your own family.*

By contrast, my grandmother was wonderfully warm and caring; she would find ways to circumvent my grandfather's designs. When I stayed in their house, I was given barley porridge cooked with water. The gray mass was placed before me without butter or sugar. "Be grateful and eat" was my grandfather's message, so I worked at it slowly. But when my grandfather had finished and gone outside to do his chores, my grandmother would say, "Now come," and she would bring out the butter and sugar.

Lesson for a boy who disliked plain porridge: Find ways to do good and make life easier for other people. Why should everything be so stark and unpleasant?

My Journey

Two or three times a year, these austere Laestadianer would come together in community gatherings known as *samling*. These were all-day spiritual and social events at which a revivalist preacher gave a stirring message and families brought their best food to share. During these get-togethers, people gave public testimonies and confessed their failings. They would publicly go to someone they'd wronged, confess their sin, and embrace that person. As a young boy, I found it somewhat strange that so many of the older men had a need to confess to and embrace the younger women in the group. It just didn't look right. My brother and I would go outside to whisper and snicker.

Lesson for everyone: It's amazing what children see. Don't discount their ability to diagnose accurately what's going on !

When the war ended, we moved from the countryside back into the city of Narvik. For the first time in five years—which meant for the first time in my memory—we could attend an Adventist church and meet people who were as "peculiar" as we were. It was wonderful!

It was there that Christ spoke to me personally for the first time. Yes, I was born an Adventist, but it wasn't until I was fourteen years old that faith became something special to me, something I "owned." I can still picture the scene clearly. My mother and I had gone to prayer meeting one evening, and we were joined by a dozen or so others, mainly women and all much older than me. There was no preacher or special speaker to stir our hearts. The Spirit had to work unassisted.

We sat in chairs arranged in a circle, taking turns reading the Week-of-Prayer material. On the surface, nothing was there that would stir a young mind—it was pretty much run-of-the-mill reading. Yet something in the message overwhelmed me, and I began to cry. My mother told me Jesus Christ had touched me, and He wanted me to accept Him as my personal Savior. And I did.

I made a second decision that evening too. I decided that I would become a preacher. In hindsight, it was an odd decision because I had a rather significant problem: I stuttered and stammered badly. But that night I set the course of my life, and over the next five years I overcame my speech impediment.

In my late teens, I went to college for ministerial training with a sense that I was wasting my time. Christ was coming! I felt I shouldn't be sitting in a classroom; I should be out somewhere telling people about His coming. But those two years in college certainly were not a waste, because it was there that I met Kari, the woman who has been my life companion. The story of what actually happened varies, depending on who the storyteller is, but out of it came two teenagers who decided to build their lives together. We were young, inexperienced, idealistic, in a hurry to get moving, and we both felt an irresistible call to the ministry. Our partnership seemed to have been made in heaven! Two years later, we married and headed full steam into the future.

Hard lessons

My lesson learning picked up speed in the years that followed. The two years of higher education became many more. I completed college and two years at the seminary when it was in Takoma Park, Maryland, and I spent a third year at Andrews University after three years of pastoral ministry in Norway. In 1962, Kari and I, with our one-year-old daughter, Laila, left for West Africa with a call to teach Bible at Bekwai in Ghana. And so began our almost fifty years of service in Africa, Europe, and the United States.

When we entered Africa, Africa entered our lives, and this bond has never gone away. Although we stayed at Bekwai for just two years, it was a never-to-be-forgotten experience. Malaria was our ever-present health challenge. It intruded unrelentingly into our lives—with particular venom in Kari's case. She contracted cerebral malaria, and it almost took her life. Although she recovered, she didn't escape unscathed; ever since then her health has been severely compromised. But in spite of less-than-full health, Kari has been an incredible partner in fifty-two years of ministry, thirty-five of which were in senior leadership positions that often entailed my traveling away from home. I could not have asked for a more supportive and committed partner, who, at the right times, has also been my fiercest critic.

I'd been called to teach students at Bekwai's secondary school and teacher training college, but I suspect the students taught me far more than I taught them. I learned to see the beauty of a culture other than my own. I learned to respect and value people who looked, spoke, and ate differently than I did. My looks I could do nothing about; the language—well, I learned a few greetings. But much of the food we came to love.

Our garden boy was a Muslim—mostly. He was earnest about his faith without completely stepping away from his primal religion. During the difficult time when Kari was hospitalized, unconscious and struggling with cerebral malaria, he fasted for three days and went to the mosque to pray for her. And then he went into the bush and offered a small sacrifice to one of the gods of his ancestors—he wanted to cover both fronts. How deeply he cared about Kari was apparent, and we've never forgotten him or his love.

Lesson for a novice missionary: A person's religion says little about his or her capacity for true caring and human compassion.

I was also the pastor of the campus church at Bekwai, and one day someone informed me that one of the teachers had married a second wife. Well, to the pure mind of a young missionary, polygamy was absolutely intolerable. I went to see him and I laid down the law. "You must separate yourself from your second wife," I told him in no uncertain terms. I didn't understand at the time that polygamy within that culture was not an immoral, promiscuous arrangement contracted because you fancied someone else. I knew little of the pressure on a family to ensure that the circle of life remains unbroken—a pressure that is especially acute if your first wife is barren.

Maybe I would deliver the same message today, but I would do it differently—I would speak with greater sympathy and kindness.

Lesson for a well-intentioned missionary: Christian values can be communicated ever so harshly if compassion for the human element is missing. Being kind is every bit as important as being right. I have found that sometimes my church is much better at being right.

After two years at Bekwai, the call came for us to move to Nigeria and join the staff of the first degree-granting college established by our church in sub-Saharan Africa. In the early 1960s, it was called the Adventist College of West Africa (ACWA). When I came to ACWA in

1964, we had an enrollment of some seventy college students and a similar number in pre-college programs. Since then it has grown into what is today Babcock University, an institution with more than seven thousand students and with one of the finest reputations of any university in West Africa. Students come from all over West Africa because they yearn for opportunities to rise, to grow, and to set themselves and their families on paths to better futures.

Lesson for a young educator: Leaders in the church have a responsibility to create hope in the hearts and minds of young people and to help them convert hope into reality.

People: The greatest challenge

After two years, the board asked me to take on the responsibility of serving as president of the college. This was my first major leadership post in the church. At thirty-one, I was probably too young for the job. I certainly had much to learn. The day-to-day running of the college—the finances, the physical facilities, and the industries—was not too difficult. The most demanding lessons I had to learn were about handling people: students, their parents, and staff. Today, many years later, I still find that *people*—not circumstances or issues—present the greatest challenges for church leaders.

In West Africa, I found the major issue facing students and their parents was finances. They had so little, so how could they possibly pay for their tuition and board? Yet the school couldn't operate if the fees weren't paid.

I still see before me a mother who came into my office to plead her daughter's case. The student was way behind on her fees, and we'd told her she could take her final exam only if she paid in advance. Her mother sat before me with tears running down her face, and I felt cruel and insensitive. Was this the most Christian way to do it? I was young and I just wasn't sure. But I felt I had no choice. I told the mother that the family would have to collect the funds or her daughter would be out of school. The mother cried until the tear wells seemed to dry up. Then a faint smile came over her face, she adjusted her clothing slightly, and she fished the required funds out of her blouse!

Lesson for an administrator in training: Reading people—their motives and intentions—is no easy task. Proceed with caution.

I faced the issue of polygamy again in the college church. I think of one man from the village of Ilishan-Remo who had three wives. Each of his wives was a baptized member of the church, for they each had only one husband. He, on the other hand, could not be a member for he had three wives.

Maybe we overlooked the principle in the matter. Maybe when a person comes to join our church as a first-generation Adventist believer, we should accept them as they are and where they are. There are some things we simply cannot go back and fix. If people have divorced and remarried five times, we consider it history. Could it be that a first-generation polygamist should be treated similarly? New standards of conduct should apply once a person has become a member of the church. But when you ask a polygamist to send away, in the name of Christ, all but one of his wives, you are sending those other wives into a very uncertain future. They may well become "public property" on the streets. And what of the fate of the believer's children— children who are the offspring of his marriages? Breaking up their home and their ties to their father seems brutal, to say the least. Even the notion of the man's keeping his former wives and providing for them, but no longer living with them inflicts another type of cruelty on these women who have done no wrong.

Lesson for everyone: People matter most. Remember that the Sabbath was made for man and not man for the Sabbath.

Of rules and punishment

Rules and their application can be so wooden and insensitive that, in enforcing them, we can inflict such unreasonable punishment on someone that we dishonor God, who made both people and rules. Leadership must always be up front about right and wrong and give clear direction as to how the church should conduct its business. But, as leaders, we must also remember that God is in the business of saving as many people as He can possibly lay His hands on. It is love that drives Him. He isn't there just to prove a point. Leaders, then, must continually ask, "How can we reach people and make them feel wanted?

Where Are We Going?

How can we communicate hope? How can we heal personal fractures? How can we offer a secure future? How can we make people feel that they are the ones that matter?"

As a young college president, I was feeling my way in many matters, and I made mistakes. My colleagues on the staff, most of whom were older than me, were critically tolerant of this young upstart, and they probably had good grounds for their reservations. This early experience, however, taught me the importance of supporting the person who has been appointed to lead. Maybe I don't think he or she is a great leader; maybe I think he or she is incompetent. But the person has been given a leadership position and responsibility, perhaps without even wanting it. I owe it to God, I owe it to the church, and I owe it to the people in charge to help this person do his or her best. It's the church's reputation—and God's, for that matter—that may be at stake.

I learned this lesson anew when I left Africa to join the staff of Newbold College in England as chair of the religion department. There I worked with a college president who had a warm, kind heart but who exercised his leadership clumsily. I vowed never to criticize him or share in the jokes that were readily handed out. I had been where he was. I knew that it's hard enough to be a leader even on the best of days, and I was determined not to make his task more difficult.

Later, as president of Newbold College, I continued to learn the often-elusive lessons of dealing with challenging people, especially young people. I met a woman some time ago who reminded me of an exchange we had while she was a student at Newbold. This particular woman had not been an easy customer to handle as a dormitory student. She tested the tolerance and patience of the dean of women almost to the breaking point.

One day, she was standing in the hallway of the administration building talking to two other students when she saw me coming down the hallway. She said to her friends, "I'm in trouble. I've gone too far this time and I know they're going to throw me out." It wasn't that she had done some particularly evil act. Instead, it was what she looked like—which was outrageous! Her hair was colored a very bright green, and I won't describe the rest of her appearance.

This is what the woman told me years later: "When you came

down the hallway, you stopped in front of me, looked at my hair, and said, 'Well, I suppose even that is possible!' And then you just walked away." I'm happy to say that in later years, this young woman became a wonderful professional and a faithful member and lay leader in her church.

Lessons for a new college president and for anyone else who deals with young people:

- *Allow young people space to make mistakes, for these are opportunities to learn and grow.*
- *Don't get frustrated by the constant questions young people raise—they're sincere, serious, and they care. Answer them carefully, because they're not pushovers.*
- *And love them. Love is the single most powerful gift we can give those who are young.*

A couple of years after we returned from Africa to Europe, I was granted a two-year study leave at Tübingen University in Germany to finish my doctorate in theology. Those were unforgettable years. We had, and still have, a warm and strong Adventist church in that city, and our spiritual family there received us with open arms. However, on the other six days of the week, our contacts—social and otherwise—were with people who were not part of the Adventist community. For my family, this was a completely new and somewhat intimidating experience. Within the Lutheran world of Germany, Adventists were widely looked upon as a sect. I took some classes from one of Tübingen's most famous theologians. When he learned that I was an Adventist, he said, "What on earth are you doing at Tübingen?" I suspect that over the years, some of my fellow church members have wondered the same!

Lessons for an Adventist administrator grappling with his first prolonged exposure to the "world":

- *People of other faiths relax when they get to know you as a human being.*
- *Mixing socially with people of different faiths or no faith is the best way to share your values and show people why you're passionate about your beliefs.*

When people like you

I discovered that when people like you as an individual, they will consider respectfully even potentially sensitive questions of theology. One day, without prior notice, a professor asked me in the presence of some twenty other students in a seminar, "Ellen G. White has a special function in your church. What is her role and her authority?" I gave my answer and stated how we see in her writings a manifestation of the prophetic gift spoken of in Scripture. They may not have agreed with me, but they received my answer respectfully and wanted to understand me because they knew me and knew I was genuine. There is a lot to be said for just being a friend.

Eighteen years in the academic community as both a teacher and an administrator came to an abrupt end in 1980, when I was elected to serve as one of the officers of the Trans-European Division. The first three years I was the secretary, and the next twelve the president. At the 1995 General Conference Session in Utrecht, I was elected to be a general vice president of the General Conference, so Kari and I moved to Silver Spring, Maryland, to begin a new challenge in leadership.

Then came an unexpected turn in my journey. The Adventist Church was traumatized by certain events, which led to my being entrusted with the leadership of the General Conference on March 1, 1999. The trauma was particularly acute among workers at the headquarters of the church. Many of them struggled to interpret what was happening, with only rumors and speculation to go by. An extraordinary meeting of the full General Conference Executive Committee was called, and together we looked at questionable activities centering in the office of the president—activities that had taken place over a period of time. The committee dealt responsibly and briskly with the matter. Some people have felt that the information available to the Executive Committee should have been published more widely after the event, but I think not. I believe the matter was managed responsibly. Activities that hurt people should not necessarily have maximum exposure, and healing must be focused on the location of the hurt, and this was done.

Afterward, there was a clear sense that we needed to leave the matter behind and get on with the mission of the church. That same desire was particularly palpable among the in-house staff. Therefore, although becoming General Conference president at this time was difficult in a sense, I experienced wonderful support from my colleagues. Everyone wanted to turn the page and start a new chapter—there was an incredible yearning to be done with yesterday and move on.

When I recall that time, I think of the words of an Irish blessing: "May the wind be always at your back." Well, I felt then that it was. And throughout the subsequent years of my presidency I have felt, though maybe not equally strongly all the time, the supporting wind of the Spirit at my back. For that I shall always be profoundly grateful.

Let me mention just one memory among many from those years: When I traveled around the world visiting with our global church family, those I met always gave me a warm and generous reception. And no matter where I went, one particular message never failed to move me. From the lips of many hundreds, if not thousands, of men and women who I'd never met, came the words: "Pastor, I mention you by name before God in prayer every day." Nothing has meant more to me than this, for it is the kindness of my brothers and sisters in Christ that has made my burdens light and given joy to my journey.

Lesson for every church leader: Prayer—your own and that of other believers—is a force that will always sustain you and keep you moving forward, no matter what happens.

Chapter 2

What Drives Us?

At the General Conference Session in Atlanta, Georgia, in June 2010, just a few days after a new president was elected, I was talking with a prominent Adventist layperson. He said, "Jan, you'll find that I'm not just a fair-weather friend." And he has been as good as his word.

His offhand remark made me think, for it contained a subtle truth—a reality that perhaps we'd prefer not to examine too closely. That reality is that even within the church, the positions we hold can sometimes make differences in our relationships. We are human, so we're not always neutral toward perceived power. Position or standing can shape the way we respond to others, defer to them, and cultivate their friendship. As much as we'd like to believe otherwise, and as much as we sometimes pretend otherwise, our church is not entirely immune to the dynamics that drive people within the secular world.

Should the fact that we've been elected to a certain position, we pastor a large, "successful" church, head up an important institution, or chair a certain board make a difference to our standing within the body of Christ? The answer, of course, is a straightforward and unequivocal No. But if we ask whether these things do, in fact, make a difference, I have to say, "Yes, they sometimes do."

Motivation for church leadership is a complex thing. In the normal course of events, service in the church is unlikely to make you rich, and there are probably easier routes to fame. In the vast majority of cases, men and women choose to give their lives to the church they love for other reasons—reasons that are pure and idealistic. For most, the call to leadership is something deeply personal and Spirit led.

Unfortunately, our idealism usually lives side by side with our humanity, so our inconsistencies and weaknesses have a tendency to corrode that which is wholesome and good. The life of an Adventist leader is often a struggle between these two conflicting parts of our nature.

Profile of a leader

I've been asked many times, "What does an effective Seventh-day Adventist leader look like, sound like, and act like? What are the most important qualities a leader should have?"

The short answer to both questions is that an Adventist leader is a person of integrity. This includes spiritual integrity, financial integrity, integrity in pursuing the mission of the church and the health of the faith community, and integrity in how we deal with the vulnerable people in our care.

Beyond this basic job requirement, though, it's difficult to compile a generic list of leadership characteristics and say they are what will *always* define a good Adventist leader. For a start, how we lead will be shaped by the unique challenges of the environment in which we function. A good church leader in North America may look and sound somewhat different than an effective leader in Korea, Ghana, or Brazil. Second, our individual temperaments mean not only that we'll bring different strengths and abilities to our work, but also that each of us will understand and express our leadership roles differently.

There's another unpredictable factor: the wonder and mystery of God at work. Leadership in the church is a sacred responsibility, and God often has a way of surprising us. I've seen good leaders fail badly, and I've seen those with little obvious leadership potential achieve success in ways I couldn't have imagined.

God is vitally interested in His people. Whether we lead a ministry in our local congregation or we help lead the global church, God has an agenda and a plan for each of us, if we're willing to be led. We have to be prepared for Him to remind us at times that "my thoughts are not your thoughts, neither are your ways my ways" (Isaiah 55:8). At other times, God's ways will seem to meet our plans, and what happens next will be incredible. These are high moments in the life of a leader.

As I look back over the past thirty-five years, I can recall outstanding leaders who have done wonderfully well and those who've been memorable for reasons other than their leadership skills. What made the difference?

Beyond individual variations of style and ability, I've noticed that every outstanding Adventist leader I've known has had a number of basic qualities.

1. Outstanding Adventist leaders have transparent motives. What is in the heart of a leader when he or she champions a particular cause, or, conversely, resists a particular idea? What goes through a leader's mind when faced with something controversial and challenging, such as the role of women in ministry or a significant reorganization of the global church's administrative structures? There will always be motives, and they will tend to display themselves along the way.

The questions we must ask ourselves are, What is it that drives me to take this particular stand? Is it a clear "Thus saith the Lord"? Am I sure? Is this corroborated broadly by my colleagues in leadership who have similarly understood the Lord, or am I motivated by a desire to continue doing what we've always done so I won't rock the boat? Am I thinking of this in terms of a "pay time" for a deal I've made with some group or some segment of the church? Am I pandering to a vocal or powerful part of my congregation? Am I being led by my desire to assert that I'm in charge, and this is the way I like it?

These aren't comfortable questions. As leaders, we must be willing to admit that we can stumble in our own interpretations and that our hearing will sometimes let us down. Leadership in the church is not immune to acting from "smelly," unworthy motives, so we must beware of selling our souls.

A division leader once told me of an exchange he had with a local pastor who had come to him with a story full of sordid details about the conduct of another church leader. This was in a country renowned for church leaders who habitually discredited each other, especially when election time was just around the corner. Typically, the "evidence" was as questionable as the accusation. The experienced division leader, instead of asking for proofs, simply asked the accuser, "*Why* are you telling me this?"

It's critically important that we're as open and honest as we can be about our motives, for this defines integrity, which is at the heart of leadership.

2. Outstanding Adventist leaders have nothing to prove. I like the advice an experienced leader once gave me: "You're in charge as long as you don't have to prove it." By this test, many a leader fails. We've all encountered spiritual dictators whose style of leadership has become more self-assertive than servantlike. These are leaders who've failed to understand that their election was not the coronation of an absolute monarch.

Whether we're elected for leadership within our local congregation or by a larger constituency, our self-images can distort and corrupt our leadership. How do we understand our roles and authority as leaders? Yes, the offices we hold may be important and respected ones, but that isn't the point. The question is, What weight do we give the fact that *we* are the ones who were chosen? Let's not pretend that we're indifferent to that and that we don't think about it. We do. So the question remains, What weight and size do we give ourselves now?

It seems that self-aggrandizement was alive and well in Ellen White's day, given the numbers of times she warned against it. "Men whom the Lord calls to important positions in His work are to cultivate a humble dependence upon Him," she wrote. "They are not to seek to embrace too much authority; for God has not called them to a work of ruling, but to plan and counsel with their fellow laborers."[1] She also warned against assuming the "prerogatives of an exacting ruler," for "God is dishonored by every such display of authority and self-exaltation."[2]

Remember that ours is not a sacerdotal priesthood. Adventist ministers and leaders don't have mysterious powers to assign people to heaven or hell. We're caretakers of the flock on behalf of the Chief Shepherd, and we're servants of the people. Therefore, any form of spiritual dictatorship in the church and any leadership that comes across as self-serving or driven by a political agenda are offensive and doomed to failure.

Where Are We Going?

Good church leadership will always have an element of softness or gentleness in it, which perhaps is simply a by-product of humility. I find "hardness," as in rigidity and insensitivity, impossible to include among the qualities of an Adventist leader.

3. Outstanding Adventist leaders "read" the community. It makes no difference whether one's leadership is in the local congregation or at the world headquarters, good leaders will be able to read the pulse of the community they have been asked to lead. What are the needs, hurts, and hopes of that group? What do they expect from their leader?

I was once asked during a televised conversation with young people in an African country, "Have you ever visited in the home of a poor person? A really poor person?" It was a question that stopped me short, for how far did I *really* understand the grinding, day-to-day realities of someone whose whole existence is defined by poverty?

We can only read the pulse of our community if we're prepared to "visit in its home"—to open up every avenue we can for communication and then listen. Really listen.

True communication takes place only in the absence of fear. Do our colleagues feel safe when they're talking to us? Do we keep their confidence? Do church members feel that they can express to us without reserve their misgivings, their concerns, and their hopes? It's more important for church leaders to pay attention to what others are saying than it is for them to speak.

As a global church, we have a wealth of position statements and policies. Whenever global leadership meets, such as at an Annual Council, it considers and votes on a variety of documents, which over the years have become a formidable collection. There are good reasons for these statements and policies: they record the thinking of the church's world leadership and provide guidelines for the church to move forward as a united global community.

However, we must always keep in mind that human beings are vastly more important than any position statements. *God* and *people* are the end points for every policy or statement. These documents are valid only to the extent that they express obedience to God and serve the needs of the family of faith. Remember, at the end of the day, God will save *people,* not statements.

What Drives Us?

It's been said that the mark of good leadership is an ability to inspire people to work for you even if they're not obligated to. This is especially true within the church, where a leader "commands" a sometimes miscellaneous collection of volunteers, not a military unit. No one has an obligation to be there—our members are all volunteers who could have gone elsewhere, but they've chosen to become a part of the Adventist community. We must never take their presence, their engagement, their financial support, their interest, and their time for granted. Church leaders who fail to understand this will have a short leadership life.

4. *Outstanding Adventist leaders have the humility to be led.* I've had my assumptions about effective leadership challenged, shattered, and remade many times over, but, through the years, I've learned that the most significant ingredient of successful leadership in our church is the humility to let God's Spirit lead.

Spiritual leading is an imprecise concept. How do we test for it? What does it look like? Is it a private, mystical process?

In this, as in all matters of faith, we shouldn't spiritualize the experience of the Spirit's leading to such an extent that we leave the intellect barren. The risks are too many. God has given us our intellects and our capacities to understand, and He expects us to use them even in matters of the Spirit, so we can find safe ground to stand on. The Spirit and the mind don't occupy two different worlds. They belong together, and a leader owes it to God and to His people to make every effort to hold them together.

Occasionally, I've met leaders who seem to imply they can best seek the Spirit's leading by withdrawing into themselves. Private prayer, meditation, and study are indeed absolutely critical, but when it comes to identifying the Spirit's leading, wise leaders will also reach out for the counsel of their colleagues. Leaders who retreat into themselves to seek a personal, God-speaking-to-me moment—an experience that can be notoriously subjective—will be perceived by others as unreliable and perhaps even manipulative.

Ellen White writes that a leader should listen to those "who have been long in the work, and who have gained deep experience in the ways of the Lord. The disposition of some to shut themselves up to themselves, and to feel competent to plan and execute according to their own judgment and preferences, brings them into strait places. Such an independent way of working is not right, and should not be followed."[3]

5. Outstanding Adventist leaders can handle change. One of the things I've learned through the countless meetings I've attended over the past decades is that there's nothing more calculated to disturb the equilibrium of a group than the possibility of change. However, change is a reality, especially within the twenty-first-century world in which we live, work, and pursue our mission. Technological change, social and political change, changes in cultural norms, economic change, generational change—the pace of change is increasing, not slowing down.

People who can't understand the implications of change and deal with it within our church's framework of unchanging values and truths cannot lead. Nothing stands still, whether within the dynamics of a local church or across the grand sweep of our twenty-five-million-strong family. If we're breathing, we're experiencing change in some form or other.

Yet, I have encountered and worked with leaders who have an unbelievable and irrational resistance to change. It's as though they believe change of any kind is apostasy or will lead to it. This is a brittle and dangerous leadership posture that threatens their survival in the church.

The future is what lies before us, so it's the only place we can go. I've reminded myself many times that it's impossible to walk backwards into the future with eyes fixed on how things used to be. If as leaders we close our minds to new ideas, we become a hindrance to the church's progress toward fulfilling its mission. We become mere protectors of "the way things have always been," and we lose sight of what it means to be leaders of God's people *now*. At the global leadership level, this attitude inevitably surfaces when we consider how the local church should function and when we consider organizational structures and ministries of our worldwide church.

As we look back, we may well say, "What we did *then* was good at the time. That was how God led us." But we must then ask, "Is this *still* the best way to do it now, and will it be so tomorrow? Or is God

34

trying to help us to see better ways to do mission and keep the church together?" A leader must have the courage to ask those questions and to allow others to examine the matter openly, without feeling threatened.

6. *Outstanding Adventist leaders realize they're not always right.* No church pastor or administrator knows and understands everything. This is such an obvious point, it seems hardly worth making—except for the fact that some leaders behave as though they do.

Every leader, no matter how broad his or her background and experience, will eventually encounter a challenge or proposal or opportunity they know little about. At this point, mature leaders, who have a fair idea of their own limits, will reach out for more information and seek counsel widely, and they will be genuinely open to new and different ways of thinking.

How will the leaders respond who believe their own knowledge and abilities should be sufficient for every eventuality? Either they will stumble forward despite being ill prepared to act, or, more likely, they will respond with a swift rejection of anything that has the potential of leading them into unfamiliar territory.

Our strength as leaders is increased, not diminished, by a willingness to acknowledge our limitations and seek input from a wide range of people, even those who hold quite different points of view. Have no fear, for Spirit-led ideas are wonderfully resilient and will eventually rise to the surface, while ill-advised ones will usually sink.

Again, the prophet provides counsel for assessing what is new and unfamiliar. She writes, "The leaders among God's people are to guard against the danger of condemning the methods of individual workers who are led by the Lord to do a special work that but few are fitted to do. Let brethren in responsibility be slow to criticize movements that are not in perfect harmony with their methods of labor. Let them never suppose that every plan should reflect their own personality. Let them not fear to trust another's methods."[4]

Adventist leaders don't always have to be right, but they *do* have a sacred responsibility to stay as close as they know how to the inspired messages of the Lord. For Adventists, this means both the Bible and the writings of Ellen G. White. The two don't have the same function, but that doesn't signify two different degrees of inspiration or values. You're either inspired or you're not—there's no halfway point. But the functions of the Bible and the writings of Ellen White are different. The problem of authority arises when counsel is taken outside of its functional range. "To the law and to the testimony" (Isaiah 8:20, KJV)—the revealed will of God as communicated through His prophets—is the ultimate reference point for an Adventist leader. We must take great care not to come adrift from that anchorage. The church community will lose confidence very quickly in a leader who, by word or conduct, discredits the revealed will of God.

7. *Outstanding Adventist leaders are faithful.* As you consider all these leadership qualities, you may possibly say, "This is beyond me. I can't possibility take on a leadership role, even in my local church. The expectations are too high. I won't measure up. I don't fit the profile of an Adventist leader, and I'm not sure about my motives."

I believe there *are* those who shouldn't take leadership positions, but probably not for the reasons you may feel disqualify you. I know of no criteria more important in an Adventist leader than humility and faithfulness. Nothing—education, professional skills, speaking skills, "pedigree," or anything else—will compensate for the lack of these two. Some people will be disqualified by their arrogance, their insensitivity and harshness, their lack of compassion for the frailty of the human condition, their inclination to sit in hasty judgment on the spirituality of some of their fellow travelers, their inability to love people with multiple shortcomings, their gone-astray theology, or—the list has virtually no end.

But when we submit in humility to the trust and choice of those who have elected us, and we vow to remain faithful to God, we've met the most basic qualifications for church leadership. From there on, we learn, grow, and do our best. That meets God's expectations, and the Spirit will be near to guide us in every way that we need guidance to function well as servant-leaders.

When all is said and done, if you want to be an Adventist leader, you must love your church—love it enough to be willing to suffer for it as you would for the truth and for the Lord Himself. You must be committed to give and to give and to ask, "What more can I give?"—for this is the life of love.

What Drives Us?

1. Ellen G. White, *Testimonies for the Church* (Mountain View, CA: Pacific Press®, 1909), 9:270.

2. Ellen G. White, *Testimonies to Ministers and Gospel Workers* (Mountain View, CA: Pacific Press®, 1923), 491.

3. Ibid., 501, 502.

4. White, *Testimonies for the Church,* 9:259.

Chapter 3

Bring Them in From the Cold

Through the years as I've talked with my colleagues and made decisions, either in small groups or in larger gatherings of world leaders, I've looked around and become increasingly uncomfortable. No, I've not felt anything amiss in *what* we've talked about, nor in the decisions we've made. Time and time again I've felt the Spirit moving strongly as we've dealt with difficult situations and planned for mission.

But on more than one occasion something has bothered me. There was an absence. Certain voices have been missing—voices that should be heard in the decision-making processes of our church.

It's important to acknowledge at this point that not every single ethnicity, language group, or "interest group" is going to have a seat at our church's global decision-making table on every single occasion when decisions are to be made. Logistically, it's just impossible. Consequently, we must continue to rely to a large extent on the idea of representation—that as leaders we represent not just our own particular set of interests but also the needs and perspectives of those who can't be with us. We must do this whether we're attending our local church board meeting or a General Conference session. But there are certain absences we simply can't justify.

Women

One of my colleagues may have felt that prior to the 2010 General Conference Session in Atlanta, I was trying to influence the church to open the door to the ordination of women to the gospel ministry. He said to me, somewhat angrily, "If anything is going to split this church, it is going to be the ordination of women to the ministry."

Well, maybe. But not ordaining women may be every bit as likely to split the church.

It isn't as though we haven't thought about this matter. During the past three decades, the question has been on the agenda of commissions; it has been discussed among senior leadership, including personnel from the world divisions; and it has been on the agenda of the 1990 and 1995 world church sessions, where it was voted down with significant margins. It has no doubt also been the subject of much discussion in various settings, formal and informal, throughout our global church.

In the 1980s, two commissions established by the General Conference met to consider this matter, one in Takoma Park, Maryland, and the other in Cohutta Springs, Georgia. The recommendations from both were that we should not proceed with ordaining women for ministry. Interestingly, however, the recommendation from the Cohutta Springs commission stated that we did not find a clear Yes or No in either Scripture or the writings of Ellen White regarding the ordination of women, and both sources affirm that there's "a significant, wide-ranging, and continuing ministry for women . . . according to the infilling of the Holy Spirit."[1] This led to a further recommendation that was approved by the 1989 Annual Council, regularizing a functional role for women in pastoral ministry.

The fact that members of the commission found no unequivocal statements in either Scripture or the writings of Mrs. White does not solve the issue for us. The apostle Paul's statements are known and used by both sides of the argument, and the canon is closed. Similarly, there is no new discovery to be made in the writings of Mrs. White. We should note, though, her many comments affirming women in service and ministry. She wrote that women "can be the instruments of righteousness, rendering holy service. . . . If there were twenty women where now there is one, who would make this holy mission their cherished work, we should see many more converted to the truth. The refining, softening influence of Christian women is needed in the great work of preaching the truth."[2]

In a passage where Mrs. White is speaking of official church workers, paid from tithes, she says, "God wants workers who can carry the truth to all classes, high and low, rich and poor. In this work women may act an important part. God grant that those who read these words may put forth earnest efforts to present an open door for consecrated women to enter the field."[3] Again, she writes, "It is the accompaniment of the Holy Spirit of God that prepares workers, both men and women, to become pastors to the flock of God."[4]

Clearly, when Mrs. White uses language such as "preaching the truth," "carry the truth," and "become pastors to the flock," she is not talking about social services, nursing in the hospitals, or teaching in the classroom. She is talking about pastoral ministry as we know it. So, where do we go from here? This isn't an issue that's going away, nor should it. We just have to find a way to resolve it.

During the years I served as president, I placed high value on preserving the unity of the global church. The strain on that unity will increase as we grow, but I believe we have an obligation to God to do all we can as leaders to hold the family together. At the same time, we must do all that's humanly possible to help the global Adventist Church be faithful to God and effective in mission. These two things, faithfulness to God and effectiveness in mission, are the forces driving our need to resolve questions about the role of women in ministry and in elected leadership.

One of the challenges of being a global community is that our spiritual values must find life within a broad range of different cultures. There will be variations—not in the values themselves, but in the way they're expressed. We're all children of our own culture. We may have ever-so-grandiose and bombastic opinions about how Adventists should behave elsewhere, but we can only express our obedience and faithfulness to God where we are. We have to trust our brothers and sisters elsewhere to do the same where they are. Will there be differences? Maybe. Should that trouble us? No, as long as our essential spiritual identity—our doctrines—are preserved.

It has become clear that parts of our world church would like to go beyond where we are now on the matter of women in ministry. For

40

them, faithfulness to God, effectiveness in mission, and just basic integrity demand that they move toward bringing women into ministry on an equal footing with men. In parts of our global church, the younger generation finds it difficult to understand why we don't fix this. They don't feel they can be part of a church that discriminates in a way that society has already moved beyond, moved to a higher standard. Should society set the church's values? Of course not. But they ask, "If the inspired pen has not provided counsel that says 'Thou shalt not,' then shouldn't we do what we believe on other grounds to be right?"

So, how do we do this?

When we took this issue to the 1990 General Conference Session, church leaders gave ownership of the issue to the global church *in session* rather than to the global church *at Annual Council*. The group that meets at Annual Council is no less global than the world church sessions that are held every five years; it's just that the group is smaller, and who attends and votes is determined in a different way. Those who meet for Annual Councils are the elected leaders of each of the church's thirteen divisions and the more than one hundred unions, as well as laypeople and pastors from every part of the world. These representatives deal with administrative issues, and they vote policies and position statements on behalf of the whole church.

By contrast, General Conference sessions elect global leadership, deal with *Church Manual* matters, amend the church's constitution and bylaws, and keep our official Fundamental Beliefs up to date. The sessions also receive reports about the progress of our work around the world, and for this reason it becomes a spiritual feast and an incredible time for fellowship.

But the delegates at a session, because of the full election agenda, are caught up in a hectic daily program. There's little time to seriously consider complex, time-consuming issues. If such an issue comes up and leadership speaks with one voice, delegates will usually vote in support of the proposal. They trust that church leaders have carefully and prayerfully considered the options and come to a consensus.

This tendency is both reassuring and troubling. If leadership is divided on an issue, the session delegates are ill prepared to resolve the matter. It becomes even more complicated when people with extreme views find their way to the microphone. In the absence of clear direction from leadership, the session is vulnerable and can be manipulated.

I see no prospect that some future session will resolve the question of the ordination of women differently than past sessions have. If the leadership of the church requests the session to transfer responsibility for this matter to Annual Council, then I believe we will have a forum that can deal with this question effectively.

I understand, but I find it troubling, that major parts of the world church say they've waited long enough and they're losing patience. I know the pressure on division leadership is severe. They're feeling the pull of competing commitments: to their global church family, on one hand, and to the church members in their local territory, on the other. To further complicate matters, we hear that a local conference may elect a woman as conference president. To me, the problem is not one of having a woman serve as a conference president, but one of a local part of the church taking this step before the ordination issue is resolved. It seems to me to be a case of the proverbial "cart before the horse." The conference president is the senior pastor in that constituency and the overseer and advisor to scores of ordained pastors. Surely something is wrong if a conference president doesn't carry credentials equal to those of the pastors who serve in her territory.

Some leaders hold the strange belief that it is easier to live with a local rebellion than it is to approve of it ahead of time—that asking for forgiveness is a better option than asking for permission. To me, this seems to be an odd administrative model, to say the least.

What the North American Division requested in 1995, which was voted down by that session, should probably be looked at again. The request was that "in divisions where the division executive committees take specific actions approving the ordination of women to the gospel ministry, women may be ordained to serve in those divisions."[5] In effect, the church in North America said, "In our territory, we're ready for it. It's our conviction that in our part of the world, we can best be faithful to God and be effective in mission if women are brought into the gospel ministry on equal footing with men."

Perhaps many other divisions of the world church wouldn't want to take this step themselves, but they would understand that, for another part of their global family, the demands of faithfulness may be different.

Young people

In November 1848, Ellen White experienced a vision that had profound consequences for the development of our church. It's sometimes called the "streams of light" vision. She saw that James White should start publishing a "little paper" that would eventually take the Advent message around the world like streams of light.[6] What is remarkable to me is not just the vision itself, but also Ellen White's actions after she received the vision, and her determination to see the Lord's plan put into action in spite of those who said it was impractical, if not impossible. She stood firm against the disapproval of other leaders, such as Joseph Bates, who felt that her husband, James, would be more effective as a preacher than a writer. She also withstood the doubts of James, who saw the huge financial difficulties involved in printing and distributing such a paper. She insisted, "He must write, write, write, and walk out by faith."[7]

It's easy to forget that she was just twenty-one years old.

Today, far too many of our young people and young professionals are not contributing to church leadership. They're leaving. As church president, I began a series of conversations with Adventist young people and young professionals around the world called *Let's Talk*. These thirty-plus conversations took place during live television broadcasts in each of the thirteen world church divisions, and through them I came to feel a deep and profound trust in our young people. Yes, there were moments when I was skeptical, but it has come back to me in conversation after conversation that *young people love this church*. This is where they want to be. This is where they want to serve the Lord. They are ready. They also have something important to contribute.

Frequently, at the heart of what young people were concerned about were the questions "Why can't we be allowed a greater say?" and "Why can't we be more involved in leadership?" These questions are demanding, but they're fair. The young people weren't asking, "Why can't more of us be members of the General Conference Executive Committee?" They weren't really even asking why more of them couldn't be members of division or union conference committees.

Instead, they want to be entrusted with a greater share of responsibility for running their local congregations.

Why should we be reluctant to let them? Look back to the twelve men Christ chose. Look back to our own church pioneers. We sometimes forget the path we've walked and the mistakes we've made. We forget that we, too, first walked unsteadily and stumbled. This is normal until our muscles are stronger and we know where to step.

We sometimes overplay the value of experience. Experience is important, but basic personality makeup is more important. How we deal with people, our capacity to love and care for the church, and our basic sense of responsibility are altogether more important than experience. If we put the right man or woman into a certain position, that person will gain the experience he or she needs. But put the wrong person in, regardless of age, and he or she will never do well.

Adults and church leaders find it easy to become impatient with the perennial questions young people ask, many of which fall under the banner of behavior and standards. Clothes, jewelry, entertainment, music, and relationships—these are some of the regulars.

The young mind can be very "legalistic" in the sense that it sees the world in sharp, distinct lines and finds safety in these boundaries. Some young people want precise formulas, and they can be very persistent. They're sometimes not comforted with "mere" principles. They're driven by a need to define themselves and the boundaries around them. They're asking, "Where do I fit into all of this? Do I even understand these boundaries and why they're here? How does a life of obedience to God express itself?"

I grew up in an Adventist home. When I reached the age of twenty, I was really quite legalistic in my thinking. I was impatient with those who said, "Well, maybe or maybe not." To my way of thinking, the "maybe nots" were problem makers. I've learned through my own walk in life, however, that there are situations in which you have to allow others the latitude to grow and develop and to discover God's will for themselves.

This approach offers trust, but it also requires great responsibility. I remind young people, "Don't take license with your freedom. Don't take it lightly."

Bring Them in From the Cold

For young people, choice of music is a recurring theme. For them, it's a legitimate concern because music is so important to them. Just look at the role it plays in any worship service conducted by young people. Their questions are serious ones, so let's be patient and gentle and remember our own journeys along the road of faith.

Some pastors and church leaders have said to me, "We need simply to tell young people how it should be, down the line, very sharply." I can only reply, "Look, these are your children, so talk to them. They're seeking a legitimate identity for themselves in the church. Help them find it. Don't drive them away. Help them understand the trust and also the responsibility that is theirs."

Young people are also frustrated by the sheer numbers of their peers who are leaving the church. During the *Let's Talk* conversations, I often asked, "Tell me, why did they go?"

The answers came back: "Well, the church is so old fashioned." "There's no sense of tolerance." "There's too much negativity, too much criticism of how we look and of our choices."

So I would ask, "What about friendship? Did your peers leave because they lost a sense of community? Were you a friend to them?"

Often there was silence, and then the answer would come back, "Yes, maybe we failed some of them too."

And I would ask, "Well, shouldn't you go after them?"

Young people should be commissioned to take greater responsibility for ministry to their peers. It's a task for which they're uniquely equipped. Let it be a defined, recognized ministry within the local church, like Sabbath School or being a deacon or elder. Let's provide young people with an official role and a degree of trust. They'll grasp it, and something new and powerful will emerge.

For young professionals, there's an additional issue. They receive trust and affirmation in the secular workplace, yet they can sometimes find the church environment stifling. They find themselves viewed with distrust, second-guessed, overruled, and ignored. Yet what a resource they represent! They're attuned to the pulse of their peers, and they bring unique perspectives to doing outreach in a postmodern world. They bring enthusiasm and skills that could be potent instruments in God's hands. Do we recognize this? Are we drawing our young professionals into leadership roles?

We're losing too many of our young people. Exact figures are difficult to find, but it wouldn't surprise me if half of those who grow up in this family lose their way for one reason or another. My message to the church is that we must trust our young people. Talk with them, listen to what they say, and show that we trust them by giving them opportunities and responsibilities. Will they get it right 100 percent of the time? I doubt it—but then, neither do we.

Trust them. Bring them in from the cold, and they will still be here tomorrow—and the tomorrow after that.

---

1. William G. Johnsson, "Committees Vote Recommendations on Women's Roles, Global Strategy," *Adventist Review,* August 3, 1989, 6.

2. Ellen G. White, "Setting Forth the Importance of Missionary Work," *Review and Herald,* January 2, 1879, para. 1.

3. Ellen G. White, *Manuscript Releases* (Silver Spring, MD: Ellen G. White Estate, 1990), 5:162.

4. White, "Canvassers as Gospel Evangelists," *Review and Herald,* January 15, 1901, para. 5.

5. "Session Actions: Fifty-sixth General Conference Session, July 5, 1995," *Adventist Review,* July 11, 1995, 30.

6. Ellen G. White, *Life Sketches of Ellen G. White* (Mountain View, CA: Pacific Press®, 1943), 125.

7. Ibid.

Chapter 4

"People From Elsewhere"

The truth of Scripture is that every human being stands equal in value and in dignity before his or her Creator. For John Byington, the first president of the General Conference, this was more than just a theological ideal. As a young man, he defied federal law by operating from his home in Bucks Bridge, New York, a station of the famed Underground Railway, helping to smuggle slaves to the freedom of Canada. Like so many of the early Seventh-day Adventist leaders, including Joseph Bates and James and Ellen White, Byington often took strong, frequently unpopular, stands on issues of social justice. Our pioneers believed they were called to help forge a community where "Jew and Gentile, black and white, free and bond, are linked together in one common brotherhood, [and are] recognized as equal in the sight of God."[1]

Why is this an issue for Adventist leaders in the twenty-first century? Because no matter whether we serve as administrators, teachers, pastors, or lay leaders, we'll be constantly confronted with "people from elsewhere," people who are not like us. Even within local congregations, we'll face challenges of integration, competing cultural values, prejudice, and strong ethnic or national identities. At any level of church administration, these things can strain and sometimes break the bonds of unity within the body of Christ.

We're comfortable with the familiar, and we're each products of our own culture, experiences, education, and country. But just as our church pioneers had to define what Christ's call for radical equality meant within their social framework, so we must grapple with what it looks like today in a world that's being transformed by the relentless forces of globalization.

Consider this: "Between 1965 and 1990, the number of international migrants increased by 45 million." Today, "roughly one of every thirty-five people in the world is a migrant," which means some 192 million people worldwide are living dislocated from all that seems safe and familiar.[2]

What caused these massive movements of people? The first major wave began in the 1950s. Migrants left their homes in the developing world, driven by their desire to escape poverty and to find better futures for their families. They came to the West for education and employment, and for many, this was, legally, a relatively uncomplicated process. They came from colonies to their colonial homelands—to countries such as France, the Netherlands, and the United Kingdom.

But as the door to easy migration began to close, desperation set in for many would-be migrants. They just had to find a way. Some made the highly risky journey in vastly overcrowded boats unsuited for the open sea. Unknown numbers of people lost their lives just attempting to make the journey. They were driven by an insatiable hunger to reach the shores of the "promised land," wherever that was in the West, and the strength of their desire made them vulnerable to unscrupulous traders in human life.

Today, not all migration is from developing countries to Europe or North America. Even between countries on the same continent, such as Africa, millions of men, women, and children are crossing borders into neighboring countries to find work and the means to keep their families alive.

And then there are the refugees. They leave their homelands because they fear for their freedom or even their lives. Some find protection under international laws and agreements. Still more cross borders illegally and are forced to exist for long stretches of time in "temporary" transit centers while their statuses are investigated and assessed. They're in limbo, caught between their dreams of secure, dignified lives and the harsh realities they've left behind.

"People From Elsewhere"

Whatever the reasons why they left, and however we define their statuses, the fact remains that there are multiple millions of people today living in countries other than the ones in which they were born. And when they move, they understandably carry with them as much of their cultures and values they can. So in their new worlds, they stand out. They look different. Often they speak different languages, eat different foods, and dress differently. They come with different religions, or, if they're Christian, they may express their Christianity in different ways. How do we as Christians relate to this?

Yes, in part, the issue of immigration touches on broad questions of public policy, economics, and politics. But it is much more than that. Each migrant is a human being whom God cares for every bit as much as He cares for you and me. And that makes this a matter for the church and for its leadership. How do we as a faith community and as individual Christians view the migrants who come into our communities and our churches? Is our unspoken question, "OK, so you had to leave, but did you have to come *here?*"

The issue comes even closer to home when we realize that multiple tens of thousands of them are our own brothers and sisters. *They are members of our church,* though they may speak other languages, bring with them different traditions, and have different styles of worship. We may have opinions about their reasons for coming, but they left their homelands for reasons that were compelling to them. Are we entitled to second-guess their motives? Anyway, they *are* here, so how are we going to respond?

Researchers tell us that Christian compassion and hospitality often fail when confronted with the realities of accommodating "people from elsewhere" within our midst. And this is especially evident among conservative, evangelical churches.[3] Why should this be? Why should Christians, of all people, find it difficult to extend understanding and kindness?

We're all children of God. No one is more or less so than others—no exceptions, no qualifications. We're equal, purchased for the same price on the cross. Do we as leaders have personal clarity on this issue? Are we prepared to defy the currents of popular feeling in order to extend Christ's hospitality to all, even to the stranger?

Where Are We Going?

The broader picture

Some may say, "But the migrant issue is just the tip of the iceberg. What about other ways in which intolerance or bigotry is evident within the life of the church?" It's a fair question. Even a cursory study of our church history reveals we haven't always had clean hands when it comes to how we've responded to the challenge of institutionalized prejudice.

One of the places where we've struggled most visibly with this is in South Africa, with its decades of systematic discrimination and oppression under the apartheid regime. Was our church a strong voice for equality in Christ during these years? Did we defy the political system to assert our belief that all men and women, regardless of color, must be treated with dignity, as sons and daughters of God? No, to our shame, we did not. In the words of Alex Boraine, deputy commissioner of South Africa's Truth and Reconciliation Commission, "Many faith communities, contrary to their central teachings, were active or silent supporters of apartheid."[4] We must confess that too often that was true of us.

The institutional voice of our church was also largely silent in the United States during the civil rights upheavals of the 1950s and 1960s. There were many acts of courage by individual Adventists, but as an organization, the church was largely content to be passive. As one General Conference president of that era wrote in the *Adventist Review,* the church can take no public position on the "race question" because it's clear that "no statement satisfactory to all could ever be framed."[5]

Being silent supporters of the status quo is a long, long way from the outspoken zeal of the early Adventist pioneers. What happened along the way?

As Adventist leaders today, we're writing a new chapter in this ongoing history. How will the chapter read? How will we deal with these "people from elsewhere" who are in our churches and in our communities? Will we sit on the sidelines, content to be merely reactive? Or are we prepared to do what may be uncomfortable or unpopular in order to be faithful to the unequivocal commands of Scripture and the prophetic voice of Ellen White?

The way forward

In the Netherlands, I've seen firsthand how the Adventist community and tens of thousands of immigrants are slowly learning to live together as a family. Maybe it reflects in part what's happening in the larger society of that country. In a very real way, we just have to get used to each other—in the workplace, in social settings, and in the church. We'll then see and experience the beauty and richness that ethnic variety brings when those involved share the greater values in life.

Leaders, especially in the local congregation, and particularly the local pastor and elders, must nurture an environment of hospitality and welcome in our churches that extends love and acceptance to everyone. I believe God expects nothing less, and I believe He will hold us accountable.

The migrants are open and they're vulnerable. "Strangers in a strange land . . . without church relations, and who, in their loneliness, come to feel that God has forgotten them."[6] We can offer them a home.

I recognize that in many countries, migrant church members tend to congregate in their own churches. There are hundreds of ethnic African, Asian, and Latino Adventist churches in North America and Europe. Being together enables migrants to maintain continuity with the cultures, languages, worship styles, and social fellowship of their home countries. This is understandable and shouldn't be discouraged—everyone needs a sense of home and belonging. However, the life span of ethnic churches of this kind is limited. The children and grandchildren of the immigrants gradually merge into the cultures of the host countries. This is where they go to school. This is where they work. They want to integrate their worship life as well.

When Adventist Church growth statistics are cited in the West, some respond, "Oh, but that's mainly among the immigrants—Africans, African Americans, Latinos, and Asians."

So what? Look at what's happening around us. In effect, the world is flat. People are on the move everywhere, and this is a fact that isn't going to change. The ethnic profiles of Western nations will never go back to what they were fifty or sixty years ago. The migrants are here to stay, and their numbers will grow. And it is of just such a mixture of people that citizens of the new earth are made. As a believing community, we must learn to be inclusive, to embrace people from elsewhere, and to be hospitable. And let's not for a moment allow ourselves to think that this is just temporary. The change is here to stay.

Putting out the welcome mat

The Bible clearly encourages us to show hospitality to strangers. The Old Testament presents strangers as vulnerable and therefore under divine protection. The Hebrews were instructed not to "mistreat or oppress a foreigner, for you were foreigners in Egypt" (Exodus 22:21). Abraham, their father, had also been a migrant and a sojourning stranger, as were Moses and the Israelites in Egypt.

The story of Lot, who extended hospitality to two strangers, led Mrs. White to write, "Many a household, in closing its doors against a stranger, has shut out God's messenger, who would have brought blessing and hope and peace."[7] Job practiced hospitality, saying, "No stranger had to spend the night in the street, for my door was always open to the traveler" (Job 31:32). And the fourth commandment itself contains a divine injunction to extend the hospitality of the Sabbath to "any foreigner residing in your towns" (Exodus 20:10).

When we reflect the spiritual value of hospitality, we bring host and stranger together and find that our differences are not as compelling as what unites us. As leaders, let's do everything we can to build communities where someone "from elsewhere" is simply "one of us."

1. White, *Testimonies for the Church,* 7:225.

2. "About Migration," International Organization on Migration, retrieved March 11, 2011, http://www.iom.int/jahia/Jahia/about-migration/lang/en.

3. See, Matthew Soerens, Jenny Hwang, and Leith Anderson, *Welcoming the Stranger* (Downers Grove, IL: InterVarsity, 2009).

4. Quoted in Jeff Crocombe, "The Seventh-day Adventist Church in Southern Africa—Race Relations and Apartheid" (unpublished paper presented at the Association of Seventh-day Adventist Historians meetings, April 19–22, 2007, at Oakwood College, Huntsville, Alabama), 7.

5. R. R. Figuhr, "A Letter From Our President," *Review and Herald,* January 2, 1964, 5.

6. Ellen G. White, *Christ's Object Lessons* (Mountain View, CA: Pacific Press®, 1941), 233.

7. Ellen G. White, *Patriarchs and Prophets* (Mountain View, CA: Pacific Press®, 1958), 158.

Chapter 5

The Church and "Other People"

S ometimes we divide the world in much the same way the chapter
title does—the church and "other people," us and "them." We
become preoccupied with reinforcing the lines of demarcation between Seventh-day Adventists and everyone else.

Is there a better, more authentic way of understanding who we are?
It's true, we're undeniably different. We're a "peculiar people" who
exist for a specific purpose. But like it or not, we're also part of the
humanity around us, and while we may have a special mission, we
have no monopoly on Christ's love.

I have an acquaintance who often invites me to visit with him and
his family when I'm traveling in his part of the world. He's a religious
man, but we don't share the same faith. In fact, my friend is a high-
level official in another church. Is this a good friendship for me to
pursue? The answer will seem obvious to some, yet the question may
give other people pause.

How should individual church members and how should Adventist
congregations relate to the world of otherness that exists beyond our
church doors? What principles should guide our relationships with
those who don't believe as we do? How far and in what ways should
we be drawn into the life of our communities?

This is very much a leadership issue, for leaders throughout our
denomination, whether in our churches, schools, or institutions, are
constantly shaping its internal culture. Are we creating an Adventist

culture that sees the world merely as a place filled with sin, a place we left behind for good when we became believers?

Jesus Christ gave a straightforward vocation to each of His followers that, like it or not, involves venturing back into the world. He said, "You are to be my witnesses to the ends of the earth" (see Acts 1:8). How can we practice our Christ-given vocation if we fear and avoid the very environment in which we've been placed for mission?

Jesus taught His disciples an important lesson on the mount of transfiguration (Matthew 17). As Peter, James, and John reeled from the sacredness of the moment they'd just witnessed, Peter exclaimed, "Let's build three shelters here, Lord! One each for you, Moses, and Elijah." But their Master had other ideas: He led them back down the mountain. Staying within a sacred enclosure, separated from humanity, was not the way forward then, nor is it for our church today.

I grew up in a home with parents whose faith was strong but from whom I absorbed the unspoken lesson that I was to be careful not to get too close to anything "worldly." Contamination was an ever-present danger. Instead, I now believe we should be teaching that faith and the presence of the Spirit will make us strong. Contamination is not a significant threat if we're sure about who we are and who walks with us.

Mission of a risen Lord

It's the *resurrected* Christ who calls His followers to be witnesses. What bearing does this have on our testimony? First and foremost, it means we're to proclaim that God is King and Jesus Christ is Lord and Savior. The Resurrection is the Father's vindication of Jesus Christ; it confirms that Jesus is everything He claimed to be. He is Lord of the universe. The reality of His resurrection gives us a sure foundation for all we do, all we preach, and all our hopes.

How can we best represent the risen Lord in our world?

So that the comments I make in what follows won't be misunderstood, I need to make it very clear that I believe public evangelism will always be a primary instrument of our mission calling. Evangelism is the appealing voice of Jesus saying, "Come unto me" (Matthew 11:28, KJV) and "Behold, I make all things new" (Revelation 21:5, KJV). Evangelism is preaching the Word of Christ and sharing biblical values in a way that helps draw people into a life of obedience and faithfulness.

Public evangelism need not mean a megaevent that packs out a local stadium. For many of those engaged in outreach, especially in the West, it may be a triumph to attract even ten or twenty visitors. We can't say whether one event is more successful than another because success is measured in faithfulness, not numbers.

Another significant variant of evangelism that has fueled phenomenal growth in the Adventist Church in South America is the small-group evangelism movement. Groups of less than a dozen church members and visitors meet to study the Word of God. Over a six- to twelve-month period, members of the group not only finish a comprehensive study of Scripture, but they establish a firm circle of friends within the church. They now belong.

Friendship is powerful. It draws people in, and joining the church can become a natural outgrowth of the strong relationships formed. It's important, though, that each local congregation ask itself, "How can we do evangelism *here*? What model would be most effective?" We should never just opt for the prepackaged, one-size-fits-all approach. Instead, we should shape our evangelism efforts to fit the society where they'll be used. And remember that any evangelism, no matter what form it takes, must rest on a preexisting relationship with our neighbors. It can't come out of nowhere. In fact, public evangelism is most effective when it's built on a foundation of practical service to our community—service that "scratches where there's an itch" and encompasses physical as well as spiritual needs.

So, public evangelism is central to our mission efforts, yet we must also accept the fact that there are places and circumstances in which, for one reason or another, public evangelism just will not happen. That leads me to ask, "What then?" What if people don't hear, by choice or otherwise, Christ's voice inviting them to learn more of Him? What about the many people who live where public evangelism isn't possible, either because of the laws of the land or because of the dominance of another religion? How do we bring a witness in those places?

And even where evangelism is possible, what about the many people who don't actually receive an invitation to come or, having received it, throw it away because they have no time or because they consider our message irrelevant? I suspect this describes the attitude of an overwhelming majority of people in the Western world toward not just Christianity but religion in general. Yet even in the "de-Christianized" West, we're still under an obligation to present the resurrected Christ and the life He offers.

During my eleven years as leader of the Seventh-day Adventist Church, I kept hearing the same question from journalists, government and state officials, and leaders of other churches and religions. They asked, "Who are you, and what do you offer to the life of my community or country?" They weren't asking for a Bible study, they just wanted to know what difference Adventists make.

In answering the question, I focused on the core values of Adventism. I told them about the broad range of services we offer to the community. I told them our church will always talk about the world to come, but we also want to make life better for people here and now. I told them that when we use the language of hope, we're not talking about just the future. I intended them to understand that our church wants to engage with people on multiple levels, and that we'll meet them where they are *today*.

At a formal reception recently, I met a lady who said, "Seventh-day Adventists! Yes, my husband was on the diplomatic staff based in Hong Kong, and both of my children were born at one of your hospitals there. The members of the staff were wonderful people; they offered the best service in the city." For her, our name carried instant positive recognition.

Adventist leaders come in many different "shapes," from local lay leaders to school or hospital administrators to pastors. But there is one element of our job description that remains the same no matter where and how we serve. We are ambassadors of the risen Lord, constantly searching for ways to share Him within the context of our own cultures and circumstances.

We have a choice: members of the public will come either to view us as a part of them, prepared to take an active part in shaping the community, or see us as an irrelevant sect that nurtures its separation and isolation.

Where Are We Going?

How can we show ourselves as ready to be part of our communities? What can we tell people about Seventh-day Adventists?

What we can say

1. Our spiritual values are bigger than time or culture. "You Adventists use the Bible a lot," a journalist said to me once during a television interview. "Do you really think modern life can be instructed by something that was written two thousand years ago? It was a different world then."

We need to be very deliberate in demonstrating how the values of Scripture transcend social structures. Our values aren't trapped in any period of history or in any culture. Compassion, selfless service, honesty, love of freedom, tolerance, respect for each other, the willingness to give rather than to take—these are incredibly powerful tools for nurturing relationships and shaping the communities where we live today. And they're values that government officials and other public leaders hold in high regard.

Our biblical values are both age-old *and* up-to-the-minute current.

2. Our values have to be lived. The values we stand for aren't locked away in codified theories, and they don't just exist in textbooks or archives. In fact, the most articulate spokespeople for our values are not academics or even theologians but "ordinary" committed men and women who live their faith rather than just talk about it.

Take just three values that have been part of our movement's history from the beginning: religious liberty, temperance, and health care. These causes are not mere addendums to our mission. We're talking here about offering people God's freedom to live and worship according to their conscience, and the freedom to live a balanced, healthy life.

I want the public to know Adventists as eloquent defenders of freedom for everyone, not just for ourselves. Since 1893, the International Religious Liberty Association, hosted at our world headquarters, has defended people's freedom no matter what their religious tradition. Similarly, our church has a strong track record in supporting temperance and speaking out against tobacco, alcohol, and the misuse of drugs.

Does the general public think of all this when it hears our name?

The Church and "Other People"

This is not really a public relations responsibility of church administration, although the corporate voice of the church should be heard more clearly and consistently on these things. The major burden here lies with the local congregation, because it's there that our values are actually lived.

As leaders, let's ask ourselves, "Are we looking for ways to get into our community and meet specific local needs?" We have men and women in our church with many different professional skills and with hearts full of compassion. Are we using them? The possibilities are almost endless: ministry to those in prison; to the deaf or blind; to those wounded by family breakups; to those whose life has been torn apart by addiction, poverty, sickness, or financial disaster. Every congregation can find a niche within its community where it can provide an essential service or resource. A church that isn't reaching outward, searching for needs to meet, will sooner or later become irrelevant to its community and to God.

I can hear some people object, "Isn't this just a resurrection of the old 'social gospel' agenda? This world is doomed and decaying, and we're on our way out. Shouldn't we just let misery live its own life and focus on getting people ready for the world to come?"

With all its flaws, this world is where we are, and this is where we do mission. Our mission is broad and comprehensive and its purpose is to reach human beings in need, wherever they are and whatever state they're in. Until our Lord returns and declares this chapter of human history over, we can't walk away from our responsibility to stand in solidarity with the human plight. This is an inseparable part of our public witness.

3. Preparing people for an unending future. With more than seven thousand schools, colleges, and universities, the Adventist education system is the largest privately owned school system in the Protestant world. Running schools has been part of our mission program since we began our work almost two centuries ago. To start with, some schools may have been intended to provide education only to Adventist children, but today many of our schools, which are all open to the public, have a majority of students who aren't part of our faith community. While the curriculum in our schools meets standards set by appropriate authorities, we provide more than just "head knowledge." We try to create an environment shaped by biblical, character-building values, such as integrity, ethics, and morality. This makes what we're doing "mission."

Why do we invest so heavily in education? Because we're committed to influencing the minds of young people for tomorrow and to helping them embark on courses of fulfilling their unlimited potential. God's never-ending future begins now, so our education agenda will always offer people spiritual, intellectual, and physical development, along with values that will last for eternity.

4. We are peacemakers. During the 1994 genocide horror in Rwanda, our church failed, as did many others. We failed because we were part of a community that considered itself thoroughly Christian, yet which failed to stop a mindset fueled by hatred. This primary failure had already taken place by the time the mass slaughter began. Then, when the violence started, we didn't provide "cities of refuge" that might have saved thousands of lives. An untold number of people died violently and needlessly because ordinary Christians failed to act as Christ would have. As a church, we must never fail like this again.

As much as I want the public to know Adventists as peacemakers, it's a description we have to earn, not one that we can just claim. When tribal or ethnically driven violence erupts, as we saw in the Biafra War in Nigeria in the late 1960s, in Kenya's more recent post-election turmoil, in the Balkan region in the early 1990s, or in a thousand other times and places we could name, we can't be bystanders. Let's never forget that in fulfilling Christ's command to be peacemakers, silence can be as much a failure as speaking the wrong words. With our silence we become complicit in evil.

Is this an issue for leaders? Without a doubt. We need to speak Christ's message of peace from pulpits, but, more important, we have to show through our actions that we oppose anything that instills hatred or inflames violence.

As leaders, we may feel we have limited tools for intervening in some of the larger, divisive issues in society, but we can consistently speak for peace, and we can demonstrate in our local congregations that Christ has the power to heal all kinds of division: personal, political, ethnic, and spiritual. Our church is global, cross-cultural, and cross-racial, and it can become a powerful public symbol of the unity, harmony, and acceptance that life in Christ brings.

The world is made up of people

I fear that our self-view of "being in the world but not of the world" may sometimes have led us to project ourselves incorrectly or to misunderstand the scope of our mission mandate. It's obvious, both in our Lord's prayer in John 17 and in many other passages of Scripture, particularly in Paul's writings, that there's a real tension between the values of the world and those of God's kingdom. It's crystal clear that the "deeds of the flesh" and the "fruit of the Spirit" are radically different in character. The church, as the body of Christ, will always differ from the world that rejected Jesus Christ and crucified Him.

But our heavenly Father "so loved the world" and the people of the world, with all the smelly mess that we've created, that He sacrificed His own Son to give us hope and a future. As His witnesses, how can we turn our backs on the world He came to save? We're not to be swallowed up by the world or be distracted by its detours from God's will, but we're to testify about God's limitless love and model the values of His Word.

Our world may be fallen, but it's a world full of *people,* and we can never walk away from them.

Chapter 6

The Church and Other Churches

Cyprian, bishop of Carthage in the third century after Christ, was a church father who had a talent for embroiling himself and others in theological controversies. More than once he took a stand that pitted him head-to-head against Pope Stephen I and divided the church of his time. One instance of Cyprian's celebrated obstinacy was his view that "there is no salvation outside the church" (*extra ecclesiam nulla salus*)—and thus only baptism within the rites of the church is sufficient for salvation.

In today's world, there is not only an abundance of non-Christian faiths—both major world religions and local primal religions—but there's also an array of Christian traditions too multitudinous to number, each with its own internal variations. They all claim to focus on God and to seek Him.

What does the God of Scripture make of all of this? Is He reachable through any or all of these traditions? Or was Cyprian right in asserting there's no salvation outside of the Christian church? Should we tighten the circle even further and say there is no salvation outside "my church"? Would that be a safe and defensible position? Would it come close to God's point of view?

This question of how God views other religions holds particular significance for Seventh-day Adventists. It's a question that touches vitally on our understanding of ourselves as the remnant people of God. It informs how we should—or should not—relate to other religious confessions, and it impacts how we understand and pursue our mission.

Among Adventists, there's a deep suspicion of anything that suggests a cozy relationship with another religious or spiritual community. "Building bridges to Babylon," "waist deep in ecumenism," drinking the "wine of error": these were a few of the more charitable descriptions I came across recently on a Web site condemning the Adventist Church's participation in a series of interfaith conversations. Paranoid? Perhaps. But amid the invective, I sensed also a legitimate question born of a genuine concern.

When we hold out a hand of friendship to other faith groups, either at a corporate level or within a particular community or town, do we somehow taint the purity of our message? Are we perhaps indulging a desire for acceptance that weakens our identity as a "peculiar people" set apart for a special mission? Should our commitment to mission and doctrinal purity keep us from getting too close to other faith communities even though they may share some of our humanitarian goals?

For Adventist leaders today—lay leaders, teachers, pastors, and administrators—the answers to these questions have practical consequences. Consider for a moment a demographic snapshot of world religions. Estimates vary, but in very general terms, Muslims make up some 22 percent of the world's population, Roman Catholics about 18 percent, Hindus 13 percent, Protestant Christians around 9 percent, Buddhists 6 percent, Orthodox Christians about 4 percent, and Sikhs, Jews, Baha'is have well under 1 percent each. A catchall category of smaller miscellaneous religions makes up about 13 percent of the world's population, while the nonreligious make up another 13 percent.

Now take a deeper look into Protestant Christianity and you'll find that of the estimated 670 million Protestants in the world, only about 17 million—less than 3 percent—are baptized members of the Seventh-day Adventist Church.

What do these numbers tell us? They tell us that, except for pockets here and there, Seventh-day Adventists live, worship, and evangelize as a "few among the many." This means that throughout much of the world, we exist in the minds of the general population as a footnote—

an interesting yet inconsequential religious subgroup. And whether we like it or not, it means that simply because we occupy space next to each other, we'll continually interact with people who neither share nor understand our beliefs.

Is our public impact as a church disproportionate to our numbers? Yes, without a doubt. Are we growing as a denomination? Yes, at a rate faster than almost any other Christian communion. Is our comparatively small size a reason for us to feel beleaguered or insecure or for us to doubt our ability to carry forward our mission? By no means. The power of the Holy Spirit to work through us is not limited by anything as humanly mundane as our numerical strength.

But the reality of our size in relation to other faith groups presents us with a choice. It's a choice between two broad attitudes, and it's a choice we cannot escape. We will inevitably come down on one side or the other, whether through conscious decision or simply through inaction. The questions is, will we adopt an open stance—engaging in a straightforward way with other Christian groups and other world religions, unafraid to speak of who we are, what we believe, and the mission that drives us—or will we adopt a bunker mentality, timidly withdrawing into ourselves and calling any communication with other religious groups "dangerous compromise"?

Over the years, I've seen the practical consequences of each attitude, both for individuals and for our ability as a church to move forward. And I've seen repeatedly the intense back-and-forth generated between proponents of both stances as they talk past each other, vigorously quoting Scripture and the Spirit of Prophecy to bolster their opposing points of view.

Why does this question of our relationship to other faith groups generate misunderstanding and suspicion within our ranks? It's impossible to say, but I suspect roots of confusion may lie buried somewhere within our shared history and identity as a church charged with a special mission. That we *do* have a God-ordained purpose for these last days there can be no doubt. But what does this mean for our inevitable encounters with those of other faiths?

It's important for me to say clearly that the question of ecumenism is not on the table. That issue has long been settled; the inspired counsel of Ellen White clearly says that the goal of uniting Christianity under one banner at the expense of diluting truth or glossing over doctrinal differences is for us simply untenable.

Through the years the Adventist Church has often sent observers and sometimes participants to meetings of interchurch groups. Yet at the same time we've stood apart, openly saying why we've done so and clearly stating our agenda. We have not compromised our identity and integrity or created expectations that were beyond reach.

There are a multitude of ways and acceptable reasons to engage in conversations with other religious groups. However, for us the big questions are how these conversations will affect our sense of mission and whether we've been true to our identity as a stand-apart Christian community.

It's an inescapable fact that the Adventist Church stands in the public arena. We have an agenda, and we want to be heard. We will not go away. So when we encounter others in the same public space—whether representing Christianity, Islam, or some other faith tradition—we have to ask what we should know about them and what we want *them* to know about us. Either we present ourselves, or others will do it for us, with the high possibility of caricature and inaccuracy. Without question, we're best qualified to speak for ourselves, but this isn't possible if we're not willing to meet others, sit down with them, and talk.

In recent times, we've had conversations with some Christian groups. The question naturally arises, then, as to whether it would be a good idea to do the same with other non-Christian world religions. I think it would. Our mission is global, and we don't have the luxury of picking and choosing the areas where we are to work or the people among whom we are to work. At some point, every Adventist leader faces a variation of this issue. It's a leadership matter, and it's here to stay.

In attempting to answer some of these questions, I come back to the gold standard of decision making for a church leader no matter what his or her assignment: Is the proposed action in harmony with Scripture and with the prophetic voice of Ellen White? Does it further our mission? Are we clear about *why* we're pursuing a particular line of action and what we aim to achieve?

Where Are We Going?

Inspired counsel

Proponents of the bunker mentality do Ellen White a profound disservice when they use her writings selectively to justify a closed-off, defensive attitude toward other churches and religions. In the overarching thrust of the prophet's words and actions, I see instead an attitude of cautious and considered openness—a careful weighing of principles within the context of specific circumstances.

Ellen White spoke about finding "common ground" with other Christians as a means of opening up further conversation. "Our laborers should . . . let the ministers [of other churches] understand their position and the object of their mission,—to call the attention of the people to the truths of God's Word. There are many of these that are dear to all Christians. Here is common ground, upon which we can meet people of other denominations."[1]

I'm troubled when I hear some of my brothers and sisters speaking in a way that suggests the only genuine Christians of this world are found within the Adventist Church. This has never formed a part of our beliefs, and Ellen White herself consistently distinguished between other denominations and their individual members. She wrote, "Notwithstanding the spiritual darkness and alienation from God that exist in the churches which constitute Babylon, the great body of Christ's true followers are still to be found in their communion."[2]

And she went even further, saying, "Among the heathen are those who worship God ignorantly, those to whom the light is never brought by human instrumentality, yet they will not perish. Though ignorant of the written law of God, they have heard His voice speaking to them in nature, and have done the things that the law required. Their works are evidence that the Holy Spirit has touched their hearts, and they are recognized as the children of God."[3]

Matthew 15 records the compelling exchange between Jesus and a Canaanite woman. She has recognized Jesus as the Son of God, and, to the disgust of those around Him, she persists in asking Jesus to heal her daughter. The first mark against her is her gender—she is a mere woman within a male-dominated culture. The second mark against her is her ethnicity—a Gentile, one who doesn't enjoy the favored status of "God's special people." Yet hear the ringing affirmation in Jesus' voice as He says to her, "Woman, you have great faith!" (verse 28).

Throughout Scripture, we see examples of individuals from outside Israel who were accepted as servants of God—Rahab of Jericho, Job of Uz, Ruth the Moabite, and the Ethiopian eunuch. Think for a moment about the implications of this. It seems to me that those who expend their energy trying to second-guess God's attitude toward people of other faiths are indulging in a spiritually arrogant and dangerous pastime. The fact that God has entrusted the Adventist Church with a special mission means simply that we need to get on with the task at hand. It doesn't mean we've become de facto arbiters of God's mind.

Underlying all of Ellen White's counsel regarding how we should relate to other faith groups is also a strong note of caution—don't compromise! We're not to "sacrifice one principle of truth."[4] And again: "We must not be exclusive as a people; our light is diffusive, constantly seeking to save the perishing. But while we are doing this our strength of influence must ever be found with the loyal and true."[5]

I like the balance expressed in a statement first voted by the General Conference Executive Committee in 1926 and later reworded and added to the *Working Policy* of our church. In it, we recognize "every agency that lifts up Christ before men as a part of the divine plan for the evangelization of the world, and we hold in high esteem the Christian men and women in other communions who are engaged in winning souls to Christ." Therefore, our attitude to other Christians must always be characterized by a spirit of "courtesy, frankness, and fairness."[6] Yet within the same statement we assert our right—indeed, our *obligation*—to recognize no limits, whether geographical or otherwise, in proclaiming the Advent message, for this is the "special burden"[7] that God has placed on us, and we must be true to our divine calling, no matter what.

Does it further our mission?

Some may respond, "OK, I understand why we shouldn't be hostile toward other faith groups, but why would we want to court better relationships with them? Why should the Adventist Church spend time and money to hold a series of conversations with another world communion? How can we justify that as an appropriate use of our time, energies, and resources?" In the local church setting, perhaps an analogous thought might be, *What's the point in pursuing friendship or cooperation with "the competition"? Isn't our outreach agenda full enough, and aren't our pastors already overscheduled?*

Does engagement with other faith communities help or hinder our mission? However much we'd like a simple, universally applicable answer, I don't believe there is one, for the answer will always be "it depends." It depends on the specific situation, the entities involved, the local context in which the church must operate, and, of course, the *motivation behind* and *purpose for* the engagement. Yes, these are difficult issues to weigh, but they're issues that Adventist leaders must nevertheless be prepared to grapple with.

Principled engagement

In the post–Civil War era in the United States, as the abolitionist temperance movement began to gain momentum as a political force, one of the most effective and well-known temperance organizations was the Women's Christian Temperance Union (WCTU). Ellen White's interaction with this group—which at the time was not without controversy—is a fascinating study of productive engagement with another Christian group. Over the years, Mrs. White frequently spoke at public events organized by the WCTU. She acknowledged the vast differences between our church and the WCTU on many subjects,[8] yet she wrote, "We are not to stand aloof from them, but, while there is to be no sacrifice of principle on our part, as far as possible we are to unite with them in laboring for temperance reforms."[9]

This approach is also reflected in Mrs. White's counsel about the proper relationship between church and state. She urged church leaders not to "build up a wall of separation between themselves and the world, by advancing their own ideas and notions." To do so would "move . . . workers to make them take a course which will bring on the time of trouble before the time" and "cut off any favors" by withdrawing "from the help that God has moved men to give, for the advancement of His cause."[10]

There is a strong strain of principled pragmatism here. She is saying, on one hand, that we have a specific mission to accomplish and doctrinal

12000# The Church and Other Churches

truth to uphold. Yet on the other hand, she is saying that this is the reality we're dealing with, and this is the world in which we must operate, so let's not unnecessarily cut off any avenues that may help us achieve our goals.

As a leader of the church in Europe and later as General Conference president, I've seen firsthand the doors that have been opened for the work of our church when we're prepared to engage forthrightly with other faith groups and give a clear account of our beliefs. This is especially true in areas of the world where there's a tendency to marginalize the Adventist Church as a cult or sect, or in countries dominated by a state-sponsored religion. In breaking down barriers of misunderstanding and helping others see our church as within the tradition of mainstream Christianity, we've oftentimes gained new freedom to pursue our mission.

Over the years, I've participated in a number of conversations with different Christian groups and I've met with leaders of different faith communions. It's a remarkable experience to sit with another Christian—a genuine believer who loves the Lord and the traditions of his or her faith—and say, "I respect you, and I respect your freedom to believe as you do; but let me tell you what I believe, and let me give you the reasons from Scripture why I believe it."

A few years ago, a group of half a dozen church leaders from another denomination visited the General Conference. They had come from Germany for a tour of the United States and wanted, in part, to get better acquainted with some "minority faiths." They were utterly amazed by what they saw and heard at our headquarters. They learned about the worldwide mission work of our church, our hospital and education systems, media networks, humanitarian work, and our ability to positively impact people's quality of life within many communities around the world.

We talked for some time, and eventually the conversation turned to some of the Adventist Church's distinctive beliefs and the scriptural basis for them. One man in particular was intrigued by our adherence to the biblical Sabbath. "You know," he said, "the overwhelming majority of Christians worship on Sunday. Don't you think you could see, maybe down the track a little, a time when Adventists could loosen up on the

Saturday Sabbath—not abandon it, but at least allow for the possibility of worshiping on Sunday as well?"

"No," I said, "that's not going to happen. Let me tell you why."

What an opportunity to tell him why the Sabbath rest is so vital to our community! What an opportunity to explain how the Sabbath belief weaves a thread of meaning throughout so many other Adventist doctrines—from the reality of God's literal, six-day creative work through to the last-day message He's asked us to tell the world!

Steering a true course

As I look to the future of inter faith relations, I see the dangers posed by two extremes. The first is that which we've already explored—a fear-based tendency to retreat from principled engagement with those who don't share our beliefs. If Adventist leaders at any level adopt the bunker mentality as their *modus operandi* for dealing with other religions, then I believe we will close doors for mission that God would otherwise have us walk through.

At the other end of the spectrum of ideas, there's another uniquely twenty-first century danger that we must address. Whether you want to call it "religious pluralism," "tolerance," or "postmodernism," it seems that globalization has spawned a worldview that prioritizes acceptance and frowns upon strong belief. As technology shrinks and flattens our world, we've seen many people become increasingly reluctant to assert ideological or absolute truths. The cry is, "We have to get along!" It has become deeply unfashionable to claim that the truth one holds is "truer" than what others hold.

Some within the so-called emerging church movement reflect aspects of this worldview in which the experience of faith becomes more important than propositional truth, and the desire to affirm and respect others' beliefs outweighs one's desire to share one's own beliefs. Postmodern thinking says that simply asserting our separateness—our "specialness"—and claiming that we have truth that we want to share is akin to a declaration of hostility. It's seen as arrogant and intolerant. For Adventists, however, the existence of truth and the reality of our special mission are nonnegotiables, so, as we go into the future, I suspect we'll have to find ways to assert truth clearly and unequivocally within a global environment that's increasingly sensitive to concepts of religious extremism and intolerance.

As leaders, we need to be clear eyed about the extent to which many within our church—especially those forty and younger—are unconsciously absorbing bits and pieces of the postmodern worldview. It comes to us relentlessly through the media and popular culture. As Adventist pastors, teachers, and administrators, we have before us the task of showing how strong belief can live side by side with respect, and how our prophetic voice can and should still sound out clearly and truly.

Civility without compromise

There's no doubt that it's far more comfortable and pleasant to keep to ourselves and spend our time talking with like-minded people. Our church, however, has the broader and more challenging assignment of engaging with people of other faiths in ways that are principled, respectful, and friendly, but that also clearly say, "This is what we believe, and it's not up for grabs." We must do this, because Christ calls us to both civility and integrity, and we must do this also for the sake of opening more doors for mission. As an Adventist leader, it will be your often unenviable responsibility to steer a true course over this difficult terrain.

The truth can withstand scrutiny. Having confidence in our faith gives us, as a church and as individuals, the freedom to interact with other Christians and members of other world religions without fear and without compromise.

1. White, "Overcoming Prejudice," *Review and Herald,* June 13, 1912, 3.
2. Ellen G. White, *The Great Controversy* (Mountain View, CA: Pacific Press®, 1911), 390.
3. Ellen G. White, *The Desire of Ages* (Mountain View, CA: Pacific Press®, 1898), 638.
4. Ellen G. White, *Patriarchs and Prophets* (Washington, DC: Review and Herald®, 1890), 520.
5. Ellen G. White, *Temperance* (Mountain View, CA: Pacific Press®, 1949), 219.
6. *Consitiution, Bylaws, and Worship Policy of the General Converence of Seventh-day Adventists* (Washington, DC: General Conference of Seventh-day Adventists, 1975), 229, 230.

7. Ibid.

8. "The W.C.T.U. Workers Have Not the Whole Truth on All Points, But They Are Doing a Good Work," *Manuscript Releases,* 18:339.

9. White, "Disseminating Temperance Principles," *Review and Herald,* June 18, 1908, 8.

10. White, *Testimonies to Ministers and Gospel Workers,* 202.

Chapter 7

The President and His Associates

The historical record shows that our early church leaders were, on the whole, a fractious and argumentative lot—opinionated, vocal, and not inclined to relinquish their point of view without a fight. Consequently, Ellen White expended a significant amount of ink over the course of her seventy-year ministry in persuading, reprimanding, and counseling her fellow church leaders. Sometimes you can almost hear the exasperation in her voice: "Tell me, if you can, what will have weight with you? Tell me what reserve force the Lord has to meet your case? You ride over all counsel, you pay not the least heed to advice unless it pleases you and accords with your mind."[1]

At other times, Mrs. White herself was forced into a defensive mode through attacks, both personal and theological, from others within the church. Reading some of the back-and-forth between the prophet and her detractors provides a fascinating study of human nature. The back page of the January 11, 1870, edition of the *Adventist Review* carries an appeal from James White in response to the ongoing campaign of criticism and innuendo: "The position and work of Mrs. W[hite] and myself, for more than twenty years, have exposed us to the jealousies of the jealous, the rage of the passionate, and the slanders of the slanderer. . . . Will those who know of things . . . during the period of our public labors, worthy of exposure, or unworthy of Christians, and teachers of the people, be so kind as to make them known at this Office immediately."[2]

As church leaders today, we'll also sometimes feel besieged and beset—not by enemies but by those who should be our closest allies. Our human frailties—whether jealousy, sense of entitlement, or simply an ungracious attitude—have an unfortunate tendency to intrude into relationships at every level of church leadership. It's a reality that's as old as the story of Paul and Barnabas and as current as next week's church board meeting.

Over the course of more than half a century in leadership, I've learned that people are both our greatest assets and our most complex challenges. Our colleagues will test and try us and sometimes take us to the brink, but we cannot function without them. Yet it has never been more important for our growing, dynamic, global church that we have leadership that can communicate and cooperate across regions and between different institutions and administrative levels. How else we can marshal and direct our collective resources for mission?

So we must each ask ourselves, "How can I, in my area of responsibility, build relationships with my fellow workers that will strengthen, not weaken, Christ's kingdom?"

Foundational values

When it comes to creating an environment that draws out the best in our colleagues, I believe there are two values of critical importance: trust and freedom.

You might ask, "What about loyalty? Shouldn't this value also be included?"

I think not. In the unique environment of church leadership, the crucial question is loyalty to whom and to what? In the business world, the leadership team is tied to the chief executive officer (CEO), who determines the direction, calls the shots, and is the one everyone expects will set the pace. But the church is not a business, and elected leaders in the church are not CEOs. The memberships of executive committees and boards collectively take that role. Elected church leaders are, quite simply, servants of the Lord and His people. They have accepted a trust and a privilege, not a right or an entitlement. Church leaders who forget this basic truth and who expect personal loyalty from their associates are misguided and can't be trusted to lead.

The President and His Associates

Let me be clear: I'm not suggesting that we're justified in undermining those who've been given leadership assignments. I'm saying, instead, that when we talk about loyalty, we should all understand that the church is the body of Christ, and our allegiance and devotion belongs wholly to Him. It makes no difference whether we are church pastors, departmental leaders, or the General Conference president—we all serve the same Master. He is the only One worthy of worship, and our loyalty to Him is unconditional.

I've encountered church leaders, at local churches as well as in international leadership, who seek and expect loyalty to themselves. How do they react if an associate or colleague is reluctant to offer such *carte blanche* personal loyalty? They will move the "disloyal" one to another assignment or to no assignment at all.

A wise teacher cautioned me as a young theology professor, "Beware of gathering disciples unto yourself." He was right. It's a profoundly risky business in the ministries of the church to establish very close personal attachments, which in turn can so easily lead to intellectual and spiritual dependence that can border on idolatry. I know of an Adventist theologian, extremely gifted and engaging in teaching future ministers, who nurtured a culture in which students were drawn too closely to him and developed unhealthy dependencies. When this teacher became, from the perspective of the church, a casualty to his own positions and thinking and his services were discontinued, scores of students and ministers who were the products of his mind also became casualties.

If you've reached the point where you both supply and evaluate the thoughts, ideas, and values of your associates, you've gone far beyond the boundaries of appropriate leadership. You must change. Should your convictions or personality not let you do that, you should, for the good of the church and the honor of Christ, step aside and let someone else take the lead.

Institutional loyalty?

The question naturally arises, "So, how does this loyalty to Christ play out in relationship to the church? Does loyalty to one mean the same loyalty to the other?"

Our loyalty to Christ is constant, unqualified, and nonnegotiable.

Our loyalty to the church makes a number of stops and adjustments along the way. Let me explain. As believers, we accept that the church, as the body of Christ, seeks to reflect the will, values, and mission of Christ. That is the church's agenda. God's Word is the basis for all of that. The attachment between the Lord and His body is unique, so in a very real sense, loyalty to Christ will express itself in loyalty to the church.

But the church is also a community of flawed, imperfect, and failing human beings. As the church passes through culture and time, it expresses itself in varied and changing ways. Humanity and time don't stand still. In this flux, it's important to remind ourselves that while Christ is perfect, the church is not. Consequently, the church may consider changes now and then that may enable it to reflect better what Christ expects it to be. The church must always be *current* as it expresses Christ's will. And Scripture, as the voice of Christ, will always firmly anchor our understanding of His will. Leaders haven't compromised their loyalty to Christ in taking our church through bends in the road to bring us where we are today. On the contrary, *failure* to do so would have been disloyalty to Christ.

What do you do with those who insist that there are no bends in the road the church is traveling, and that it must never change?

Men or women who don't have the suppleness of mind or personality to cope with change cannot safely be given leadership in a church that operates in a global context. They inhabit an unreal world and have an irrational resistance to anything that looks or sounds different from the "way we've always done it." In that state of mind, they'd prefer to turn the church around and have it walk backwards into the future with them, while quoting a famous saying: "We have nothing to fear for the future, except as we shall forget . . ." But they refuse to face the future. This blindness begets a closed, frustrating leadership style, while loyalty to Christ, on the other hand, produces leaders who are both faithful and fearless.

Working with what you have

Lay members often wonder how the church's elected leaders got the positions they hold. How does the church seek out the most competent and committed men and women for key roles?

The President and His Associates

Winston Churchill once called democracy the "worst form of government—except for all those *other* forms that have been tried from time to time."[3] Similarly for our church, which must operate in an imperfect world, the processes we have are, at the very least, better than the alternatives. (In the next chapter, we'll take a closer look at these processes.) Church elections mirror representative democracy in that representatives of the constituency concerned have voice and vote. These representatives choose the senior leader and then will generally listen with courtesy to his or her suggestions about the composition of the rest of the leadership team. There's wisdom in this. It's important that the "chemistry" in the team is right, and the skills and gifts each person brings will be complementary to the whole.

I've experienced this process firsthand at both the division and General Conference levels. At the 2000 General Conference Session in Toronto, Canada, I came to the election process having served for just a year and a half as president. Once I was reelected, the nominating committee, following the usual practice, invited me to sit with it for the remainder of the nominating process. This committee of slightly more than two hundred men and women was broadly representative of the global church, and as a body it felt strongly that the General Conference leadership team should reflect this diversity. But the group was equally concerned that the president should have a team he could work with, and so we worked together to do the best we could to reflect both of these goals. My experience is that a nominating committee will not give you all you want, but it will go a very long way toward accommodating your wishes if you can provide a sound rationale for them.

Will our colleagues always be the best qualified and most suited to their assignment? Most of them will, but not all. As I look back over three decades of world church leadership, I can recall both good and poor leaders. Of the good, there have been some of the finest leaders our church has been privileged to have. They're the ones with creative minds, excellent leadership skills, and compassionate hearts. They're the men and women you turn to when you must assign difficult tasks. Their love and loyalty to Christ and His church are never in question. They have proven track records, which provide you with a reasonable basis for thinking they can get the jobs done. And they're not mavericks.

They will keep you, as leader, in the communication loop.

I've also had to work with associates whose love and loyalty were not in question, but whose minds seem to be in a constant resting mode. Such leaders will never surprise you. Their minds seem never to give birth to new ideas, and they probably wouldn't be able to assess ones should they see them. Their greatest gifts seem to be to bless that which is already blessed. They probably became part of the leadership team for reasons other than their leadership skills.

Then there are those associates whose default position is that of suspicion regarding all new ideas and proposals. Such leaders see problems where there are none, so they themselves become a problem. There's a negative quality about them. Maybe it's narrow-mindedness. Maybe it's fear. Maybe it's lack of self-confidence. Maybe they burned their fingers once too often along the way. Or maybe their upbringing as children was too restrictive and manipulative. Maybe . . .

Building a safe haven

And so we find we've been given a team of colleagues to work with, and work with them we must. Few of us, whether we're local pastors, college administrators, or departmental directors, have the luxury of picking and choosing all the members of our team. I would suggest that the place to start in building any sustainable working relationship is *trust*—the kind of trust that doesn't micromanage, that gives an assignment to a colleague and believes it will be done, and that doesn't comment negatively to others about the quality of a colleague's contribution.

Trust demands that if someone's performance has not reached the expected standard, then this is a matter between the leader and that person—and no one else. Since we will be judged by the quality of our team's work, it's in our interest to help them do better. If they will not or cannot, then let's help them move on to some other assignment. The needs of the church must ultimately be given greater weight than consideration for an individual who has been given the wrong assignment.

And there must be freedom, because if freedom is denied, the atmosphere quickly becomes suffocating. It's the leader's responsibility to provide a safe place within the leadership team where thoughts and ideas can be birthed and tested. I hold freedom to be a sacred value, yet it is so vulnerable to abuse. As leaders, we can be tempted to deny or restrict freedom in the interest of keeping things moving predictably and smoothly.

Our church is a very conservative community, which means, among other things, that we rarely depart from the familiar. Freedom of thought and expression among the leadership team allows for the testing of unfamiliar ideas in what is perhaps a safer, more disciplined environment than many other settings provide. Whether we're leaders in local congregations or at the world headquarters, the ultimate test for any new idea must be, "Is this good for the church? Does this make the church a more effective community in mission? Does it make the church, as the body of Christ, a more compassionate community?" If the answer to each of these questions isn't a resounding Yes, then the proposed course is misguided and should be abandoned.

In this environment of freedom and trust, a colleague must feel safe to talk with the leader about anything that's on his or her mind, knowing that the confidence will be honored and will not show up in corridor talk the next day. Thinking men and women, especially as they're given new and sometimes daunting responsibilities, often work with unfinished ideas. They may hold some positions tentatively or just want to test the waters. They may have serious reservations about proposals that are already being considered, or they may have doubts—possibly even doubts about the way a certain statement of faith is worded. In my view, it would be a grave failure of leadership not to provide a safe haven for colleagues to talk about whatever is on their minds. If you then compromise the trust of a colleague who has opened his or her heart to you, you've fatally compromised yourself as a leader.

When the bond of loyalty breaks

Trust and freedom are values that form a strong foundation for interpersonal relationships between fellow leaders, but loyalty belongs to a different category. Loyalty expresses itself as a leader and associates together focus outward on the same object—namely, the Lord and the mission He has entrusted to His people. He is the One to whom we all owe an uncompromised loyalty, and all of us will ultimately have our moment of accountability.

What happens when these values are seriously breached—when trust and loyalty are irreparably compromised?

I was a doctoral student in the Protestant faculty at Tübingen University in Germany in the late 1960s and early 1970s, during which time Hans Küng, a renowned theology professor, taught in the Roman Catholic faculty. He had a brilliant and versatile mind that was leading him irrevocably toward a breaking point in his relationship with his church. Professor Küng had been appointed by Pope John XXIII to serve as an expert theological advisor to the Second Vatican Council of 1962 to 1965, which opened the Catholic Church to other Christian communities and to the secular world.

The next pope, Paul VI, had a different agenda. The doors that had been opened by the Second Vatican Council were shut. Küng (and many Catholics with him) felt the credibility of the Catholic Church had been seriously compromised, and he made no attempt to keep his criticisms private. Many Catholic leaders tried to bring the gifted theologian back into the close embrace of the Roman Curia, but it was not to be.

The breaking point came in 1968, when Pope Paul VI came out with the encyclical *Humanae Vitae,* which condemned contraceptives as a grievous sin. Hans Küng's subsequent book, *Infallible?,* challenged the papal magisterium and made the gulf between himself and the Vatican unbridgeable. His attack had been too direct and too comprehensive. There clearly was no way back.

The curia responded by withdrawing Küng's credentials for training Catholic priests, perhaps hoping to destroy him as a theologian. If so, they were disappointed. If anything, Küng has since reached higher acclaim as a theologian and professor.

I remember my own thoughts at that time, and what I suspect were those of many others too: *How wonderful that one of the Catholic Church's most gifted theologians should give the Vatican a "black eye."* Yet, on reflection, what choice did the Vatican have other than to remove Küng from his lofty role as a teacher of Catholic theology to Catholic students and priests-to-be? Theology aside, Professor Küng had made his position untenable purely in terms of employment ethics. How can you represent that with which you're clearly out of harmony and obviously no longer support?

Against that background, I return to the question: How do we deal with colleagues in trusted positions who have compromised their loyalty to the church? What of a theologian like Hans Küng—high-profile and gifted—whose theology has drifted significantly from what we stand for as a church? And what about the scientist who can't reconcile scientific findings with the faith of the community he or she represents? If you've tried to find reconciliation but to no avail, what must the church do?

We've had learned men and women in our own church during the past few decades who have been in such positions. Employmentwise, there really is no choice. Regrettably, it has to come to a parting of ways.

Similarly, what does the church do when a senior elected leader in the church has seriously compromised himself or herself ethically, morally, or financially? When trust and loyalty have been sacrificed on the altar of self, the consequences are inevitable. In terms of employment ethics only—and there may be more considerations than just this—what must be done is clear. The person must go.

Trust and freedom live together, and they must discipline each other. Protecting this trust is an expression of the leader's loyalty to Christ and His body.

1. Ellen G. White, letter to E. P. Daniels, August 6, 1886. See also *Testimonies on the Case of Elder E. P. Daniels* (Pamphlet 96), 76.

2. James White, "Will They Respond," *Advent Review and Sabbath Herald*, January 11, 1870, 24.

3. 444 *The Official Report,* House of Commons (5th Series) (November 11, 1947), 208, 209.

Chapter 8

Choosing a Leader Isn't Easy!

My wife, Kari, spoke at a General Conference staff worship a few days after we returned to Maryland following the 2010 session in Atlanta. She joked that of the past three General Conference sessions she'd attended as the president's wife, the one she had thoroughly enjoyed without reservation was the very first—and her enjoyment of *that* one abruptly diminished once the nominating committee began its work. Why? In part because she saw firsthand the turmoil and sometimes pain that our church's electoral process can bring to individuals and their families—faithful servants of the Lord who've submitted themselves to be led by the Spirit and by the will of their fellow believers.

Beneath the dry language of the documents that describe the way we choose our elected leaders, from local church elders to General Conference officers, there lies a world of human feeling. There's the often anguished soul searching of those who will discuss these decisions and ultimately make them. ("Are we moving in harmony with God's will?" "How can we choose between two equally qualified and committed individuals?" "Have we made the right decision?") Then there's the courage of those people who say, "I will allow this group of men and women to decide where and how I will serve the Lord." And finally, there's an assortment of other emotions that have more to do with our humanity than with our spirituality—ambition, envy, self-seeking, and pride.

Choosing a Leader Isn't Easy!

Army of volunteers

We're a community called by God, but that doesn't make us an easy community to lead. The dynamics of leadership become complicated in an organization such as ours—an organization comprised of volunteers who can come and go at will. Church leaders have no power to inflict consequences on "offenders" for their "noncompliance." They can't fire people as a corporate executive does; nor can they, like a priest, "assign" people to heaven or hell. And the church's electoral processes mean that it's the volunteers who exercise power over leaders, not the other way around.

Being a leader in the Adventist Church carries no job security. Leaders are often overworked, overstressed, underpaid, and vulnerable to abuse. Does this mean the experience of being a leader in our church is all "tests and trials"? No, it can be wonderfully fulfilling. For me, the past three decades have been years of exceptional satisfaction. The difficult moments have tended to fade quickly from my mind, and the experience of serving God's people has been richer than I can adequately convey in words.

The path of an Adventist leader, though, is seldom uneventful, and this is especially true when it comes to facing an election, regardless of whether this takes place at a world church session, within a local church, or at any level in between.

Grassroots power

It's somewhat ironic that the units with the greatest autonomy within the Adventist Church are those that are sometimes placed at the base of our organizational flowchart. Local congregations have more scope for independent decision making than any other administrative entity within the global church. Congregations decide who will serve as their leaders and whom they'll accept as members, and these decisions can't be changed by a "higher" level of administration.

What considerations, then, should guide the decision making of a local congregation?

There's no science for electing men and women to serve as local church elders. What made you choose this one and not someone else?

What did you look for and what swung the balance for you in this choice? It's sometimes hard to say.

It's clear that leaders in a local church must have a variety of talents, gifts, and skills. Elders must be able to organize both themselves and others. They must be good communicators, both in listening with understanding and in making themselves understood. They must be willing to donate significant amounts of time to the church, and they must have a clear understanding of the Bible and of what constitutes the Adventist quality of life. And all these qualities must be immersed in a deep, uncompromising loyalty to God and to His people.

Is that all?

Important as each of these is, rising above and beyond any of them is the need for all the elders to have an immense capacity to *love people*. When it comes to leadership in the local congregation, every other skill or qualification has little value apart from love. And it's important for us to remember that this love must be extended not just to the group of believers as a whole, but also to the often motley assortment of individuals who make up Christ's body. This is not straightforward or easy. It is far less demanding to love the "many." As the saying goes, "I love humanity. It's just some oddballs among them that I can't stand."

Elders will always find a fair number of individuals in their congregation who are difficult to handle. Maybe their personality or some weird conviction makes them a strain on every social engagement. Perhaps they simply rub us the wrong way. As elders, we're not required to build our social lives around difficult people, but we *are* required to look out for them, minister to them, and treat them with unfailing courtesy and kindness. Whether we rebuke them or affirm them—and there may be days when we'll do both—they must know that we care for them. We shouldn't accept the responsibilities of being local church elders if we fail the love test, and this is not just because we won't adequately serve God's people, but also because we will find the task joyless and stressful.

Local conferences and unions

As we move beyond the local church context, there is one reality that every leader must understand and remember: *we have been elected by the few, but we serve in the interest of the many.*

Here's how it works. Each local and union conference sets out its electoral process in its constitution and bylaws and describes how their respective constituencies will participate in elections. The main constituencies of a local conference are not individual church members but the local churches as communities. In their constituency meetings, the individual members of a congregation speak and vote on behalf of all the other members of their local church family.

Basically the same is true of union conference constituency meetings—the main constituency of a union is the local conferences (or fields or missions), whose executive committees have chosen delegates to represent them at the session. Some representatives from various church institutions along with a limited number of individuals from the next higher organizations will also attend to act as counselors.

So, elections at every level of administration within the church are directly linked by a thread of representative participation that originates from the local church. Yes, these are "business" meetings. Yes, they're governed by rules and defined processes. But think for a moment about what's really going on here. As we participate in these elections, we're reaffirming the bond of our spiritual family. We're saying that we're committed to staying together, consulting together, pursuing our mission together, and working through any differences that arise.

But I come back to the reality that we, as leaders, must keep in mind: not *every* member of the Adventist Church attends the meetings at which their representatives are elected, or consents to the decisions those representatives make. However, we owe service to *all* God's people—not just to those in our flock who are vocal or powerful, and not only within the constituency that elected us, but also to every other part of the body of Christ no matter whether that part is located in the next city over or in a country on the other side of the world. We're all responsible for the care and unity of all the members of our faith community.

As leaders, we need to remember that the constituency that elects us will hold us accountable for some of our actions, but God will hold us accountable for everything we do.

Measuring spirituality?

When it comes to the personal qualities of a union or conference leader, we must briefly return to the difficult-to-measure and difficult-to-handle quality we call "being spiritual." This invariably comes up in connection with the election of leaders. The admonition is, "Be sure you choose a leader who's spiritual." And of course we must. The work of a leader is spiritual, and only spiritually alive men and women can attend to the needs of the flock. The problem comes when we try to define what a spiritual person looks like.

People differ greatly in the way they express themselves. Some are given to a generous use of a "spiritual" vocabulary, which conveys an aura of devotion. Others do not burst forth as readily and may consequently be judged unfairly. Only the One who knows our innermost being and our unspoken thoughts knows whose spirituality is genuine and sustainable.

Hence, we need to consider this in deciding who will make good leaders for the church. We need to look for a generous blend of qualities—people who are spiritual, reasonable, pragmatic, and common sense. Seek wide for opinions. What reputations do the potential elders have in the community? What do their track records look like? Do they understand the very basic challenges of everyday living as experienced by the young as well as the old? Do they gossip or are they protective of the personal information they hold? Can you really trust them?

Yes, when electing leaders we must always ask whether they are spiritual—but let's also ask whether they will operate within our church's broadly established rules or tend to make their own rules as they go along. Will they respect and uphold the policies the church in council has agreed to? Will they seek the counsel of their colleagues and the larger faith community, or will they tend to act because of private "inspiration" or by convictions that have arrived during the night season? Will they have the grace and strength to hear those who think differently?

World church leaders

It's important to understand the process we use for electing division and General Conference leaders, too, for this process impacts the ultimate choices we make. Every five years, the General Conference meets in session to elect the team that will provide leadership for the world church. This selection process is channeled through a nominating committee. Before each session begins, the divisions (currently thirteen) know how many representatives they'll have on the nominating committee. They don't actually select their representatives on that committee, though, until the first day of the session. Then, delegates from each of the divisions and delegates from the General Conference entities meet together in caucuses to select the men and women who will represent their territories on the nominating committee in the process of choosing world church leaders. The newly constituted nominating committee then sets to work, and, throughout the session, sends the names of proposed leaders to the floor of the session to be voted on by the larger body of delegates.

In the past, this process has worked quite well. However, I know from both personal experience and the testimony of others that *lack of time* is a critical factor that can seriously compromise the work of a session nominating committee. Much must be accomplished in such a short time.

I was a member of a General Conference session nominating committee prior to becoming a division officer, and I've twice sat with the nominating committee in an advisory role as General Conference president. I've noticed that at a certain point, a general fatigue sets in, and the members of the nominating committee begin to focus more on getting the job done within the time they have left than on choosing the best possible candidates for the positions they still have to fill. Maybe by then time has run away from the committee, or maybe the committee members' appetites for speeches has been satisfied, and they begin to send unappreciative looks in the direction of someone who asks too many probing questions. This raises a number of concerns for our election process, but I'll limit my comments to just two that I've observed and that have lingered in my mind long after the nominating committees' work had ended.

Politics

I wish I could unequivocally declare that there's no politicking within our church's election processes, but there is. Even months in advance of a session, segments of the constituencies that will have members on the nominating committee can hold informal consultations and agreements between people who are considered to be candidates for particular offices. Promises can be made and deals offered. Notwithstanding promises to keep the work of the nominating committee confidential, its members will sometimes talk. Such maneuvering becomes particularly apparent when we see segments of the nominating committee voting in blocks.

It may be unrealistic to think there should be no prior thought or consultation. The time available to the session in which to make leadership decisions is so short—usually four or five days—that it's understandable that some advance thinking and talking will take place. Perhaps it's more a question of how pure our hearts and motives remain, and whether we've compromised our commitment to let the Spirit lead.

Politicking, however, becomes offensive when an individual or those acting on his or her behalf create machinery to "sell" him or her. When this happens, we compromise the unfettered freedom each member of the nominating committee should have to consult his or her own experience and convictions when casting a ballot. And what about the fervent and earnest prayers we offer, asking the Holy Spirit to guide our thinking and choices? We can't have it both ways. We can't go into a voting session with our mind locked in place by an existing agreement and still appeal to the Spirit to guide us.

Representation

The extraordinary growth of our church over the past decade has made the issue of representation in electing world church leaders both more complex and more important. How can we ensure that our nominating committee, both in its composition and in its recommendations, is fairly representing our incredibly diverse global community? One way to assess how well the process works is to look at the personnel who currently serve at our world headquarters. Doing so suggests that while we've made progress, we still have some distance to go.

The need for fair representation raises other questions as well.

Choosing a Leader Isn't Easy!

Should representation be based on numbers alone? Take one specific scenario that we may face within the next ten years if we're still here on earth. Given the growth we're experiencing in Africa, it's only a matter of short time before Africans will comprise half or more of our global membership. What will happen if this is immediately translated into corresponding representation on the nominating committee and this results in nominations heavily weighted to that continent? Is our leadership there able to read accurately and understand the leadership needs of a *global* community and choose leaders accordingly?

The potential of this happening doesn't invalidate the concept of all of our members having fair representation, but it *does* mean that numerically based representation is not adequate. We need to allow other factors to help shape our electoral system so the weight of participation will be spread more broadly.

I like the models used by the United States Senate and the United Nations. California has two senators, and Vermont, with just a fraction of the population of California, also has two. Similarly, in the United Nations, the smaller nations have a voice in the General Assembly, along with the more populous nations. This arrangement assures that the entire community of nations is served fairly; the "weak" as well as the "strong" having a place at the table of leadership.

Could this concept help us as we struggle to make the electoral processes of our global faith community as fair as possible? I'd suggest, for a start, that the composition of the session nominating committee should be redefined and recomposed. Yes, I could make specific suggestions for how to do this based on my observation of how the system works in practice, but this is not the time or place to do that. Suffice it to say for now that it must happen sometime.

Choosing our leaders, whether within our local church or in any other context, is not easy. But notwithstanding its shortcomings, the best electoral process is one that is democratic and that also maintains broad-based representation. Our current system holds these ideals, but we must be prepared to look at our electoral processes occasionally with fresh eyes and perhaps fix bits and pieces that don't work well. We need to do what we can to ensure that our fallible human system is protected as well as possible from manipulation. We owe this to the millions of church members whom we collectively serve, and we owe it to our Lord.

Chapter 9

Unity—Being *One* Body

When you talk with the secular media about the Seventh-day Adventist Church, you quickly discover two realities: most journalists have little to no knowledge about who we are and what we stand for, and when a reporter *does* know something about Adventists it's usually defined by the ways we differ from "mainstream" Protestantism.

For the eleven years I served as General Conference president, talking to the media was an unavoidable part of my job. I spoke to journalists on the sets of talk shows, at press conferences, in one-on-one interviews, and on the tarmacs of airports from Mozambique to Peru. It wasn't always a comfortable experience. How do you encompass, in just a few sound bites, the depth of what your faith means to you personally? How do you communicate to someone who may have little interest in religion, let alone our church, the life-transforming power of what Christ offers? But engaging with the media can also be an enlightening experience. It forces you to see yourself and your faith through the eyes of someone else, and in doing so, you discover some interesting things.

On January 28, 2008, I sat on the set of Bloomberg's *Night Talk* program in New York City with journalist Mike Schneider, taping an interview that would be broadcast across North America, Europe, and Asia. Schneider was interested and engaged, but then he was a veteran reporter and there was nothing I was going to say that would unduly surprise him—at least until in one of the breaks we began talking about the global hospital and education systems of our church. To him, the fact that the Adventist Church was capable of developing and sustaining such vast networks was a revelation. It was amazing. How could it be possible that the Adventist school system is the largest Protestant education system in the world? How is it that our international contributions to health care and humanitarian work seem so disproportionate to the size of our church membership? And by looking through his eyes, I saw again the wonder of something that we, as Adventists, can so easily take for granted.

The origins of our church's global infrastructure, of course, lie in our system of governance, which is unique in Protestantism. We're not a loose collection of national churches that speak, act, and govern themselves independently. We're one body, whose leadership comes together regularly from every part of the world to consult with each other, pray with each other, and to be ruled by the counsel of all. Consequently, the smallest congregation in rural North America has direct ties to a house church in Cambodia, a café church in the Netherlands, and a congregation in a remote highland village of Papua New Guinea. We have an essential "sameness"—a common spiritual DNA—that you will always find if you dig beneath the surface differences of culture and nationality.

Unity of what?

When Adventist leaders begin talking about unity, some members become nervous. What exactly does *unity* mean? Is the word simply code for a rigid uniformity that allows no freedom for individual thought or expression? Is it being used to justify a top-heavy organizational structure that draws resources away from the local congregation? Or, at the other end of the spectrum of ideas, does a call for the unity of believers have some kind of ecumenical overtones?

Notice the words of Jesus Christ as He neared the end of His ministry on earth: "I pray also for those who will believe in me through their [my disciples'] message, . . . that they may be one as we are one— I in them and you in me—so that they may be brought to complete unity. Then the world will know that you sent me and have loved them even as you have loved me" (John 17:20–23).

The unmistakable thrust of Jesus' words is that those who share faith are to be bonded together as one in Him. As incredible as it seems, He is explicitly inviting us to share in the community of the Trinity. Through our relationships with fellow believers, He's calling us to reflect, however dimly and hampered by human frailty, the oneness that He experiences with His Father and the Spirit.

I don't see this as an endorsement of an ecumenical agenda. We aren't entitled to read into this prayer of Jesus any idea of maximum accommodation for everything that carries the name *Christian*. But clearly, those who "through their message" have been brought to a shared faith in Jesus Christ are meant to be united. They're one body.

There is no end to the reasons why being one body is difficult and can be a testing experience. Any organization that attempts to bring people together under one banner will inevitably run up against the realities of humanness—the fact that each of us is the product of a unique set of experiences and cultural norms. Ask any local church pastor, and he or she will tell you that those differences can be just as pronounced between people who live in different suburbs as between people who live on different continents.

Building blocks of unity

On the back of coins minted in the United States appears the Latin phrase *E pluribus unum* (out of many, one), a recognition of the hard-won agreement between independent American states to form one nation. The European Union chose the motto *In varietate concordia* (united in diversity), acknowledging the pledge of its member countries to cooperate in spite of vast differences of culture and language.

For nations, or federations of nations, unity is built largely through appeals to common material interests—the promise of shared economic prosperity and greater regional security. How does a faith community such as ours build a sense of unity that transcends allegiances of culture, nationality, and language? What values guide us, whether within a local congregation or in global church governance, in dealing with differences and preventing fractures in the community of faith?

In Ephesians 4, the apostle Paul appeals to us to make every effort to preserve the unity that the Holy Spirit is present to accomplish.

Again, we see the symbolism of a "body" with Christ as its head, and "from him the whole body, joined and held together by every supporting ligament, grows and builds itself up in love, as each part does its work" (Ephesians 4:16).

It's important to note the four qualities Paul says must be present in the church for it to have unity that works. He says the members must be humble, be gentle, be patient, and bear with one another in love. What do these values mean in practice?

Humility is a profoundly Christian value. While secular society is inclined to talk about power and greatness, Christ presents humility as the virtue on which almost all other virtues depend. Humility has to do with truly knowing ourselves. It's about seeing our weaknesses and flaws and acknowledging our failures in both relationships and actions. It means our finding no grounds for self-admiration or self-congratulation. Humility means that we don't compare ourselves to our neighbors or friends; instead, we place ourselves next to Christ—the ultimate standard. When we do that, there's no room left for pride.

Gentleness, or *meekness,* is difficult to describe. It's not weakness. It may hint at submissiveness or subservience, but gentleness is not necessarily lying down and taking anything that comes. Gentleness may even contain indignation or anger for the right causes and at the right times. A gentle person sees what's happening round about and will take exception to abuse, insults, and wrongs done to another person.

The Greek word that Paul uses in this passage suggests that gentleness or meekness is the ability to find a balance between extremes—neither too much nor too little. But there's another meaning to the word that we should note: gentleness is a quality exhibited by an animal that's been trained to obey the commands of the one who holds the reins. As a Christian virtue, then, gentleness isn't a matter of self-discipline. It's a matter of having submitted to God's control. Paul is saying that a community of believers doesn't run its own course. God is in charge, and we must submit to Him.

The third quality of a unified Christian body is *patience,* sometimes translated as "long-suffering." This word names the spirit that never gives in nor gives up, but that endures to the end. It doesn't concede defeat. It's the spirit that will not be broken by misfortune, suffering, disappointment, or discouragement. It persists no matter what.

The Greek word for patience also carries with it the idea of restraint in the use of power. It describes a power that can take revenge but chooses not to do so. This patience does not avenge wrongs or retaliate. It bears insults without bitterness. In the words of theologian William Barclay, this patience is "the spirit which can suffer unpleasant people with graciousness and fools without irritation."[1]

When we recall how often the Bible speaks of God as "patient" and "long-suffering," it's clear we're seeing a pattern of leadership that we must strive to reflect if we're to cultivate unity in the body of Christ.

The fourth value that we must have is the ability to *bear with one another in love*. When it comes to preserving unity in the church, there's no way to overstate the importance of this kind of love. The love Paul speaks of is an attitude of selfless benevolence toward others. It means acceptance and support. It means that we'll never knowingly hurt someone else. It's much more than a warm feeling, and it engages more than just our emotions. We're talking about a radical love that actively seeks to do good—even to those who may not like us or who, in our view, may be difficult or cantankerous. It's love based on choice rather than sentiment. We *choose* to live in a way that seeks the best for other people, regardless of how they feel about us. Needless to say, it's also the kind of love that's easier to describe than practice.

Building on these four values, Paul develops his argument. He reasons that if there's one body of which Christ is the head, one Spirit that is the gift of Christ to His people, one hope that fills us with a longing to reach our goal, one faith that expresses itself in complete surrender to Jesus Christ, and one baptism that follows our acceptance of Jesus Christ and marks our entrance into the church, then surely this affirms that the One God whom we worship is the Father of us all, and that bond binds us together. This is the spiritual basis for our unity as a community of believers. As Adventist leaders, whether in local congregations or other organizations, we're responsible for deliberately cultivating a climate in which this unity will grow.

Values to live by

At the 2000 General Conference Session in Toronto, Canada, the church voted to accept three strategic values—growth, quality of life, and unity—that would help shape and guide all the church's activities. *Growth* focuses in part on evangelism and outreach, an emphasis that over the past eight or nine years has seen at least a million new members added each year to the church around the world. But growth also means spiritual maturing—of individuals and our community as a whole. None of us is a finished product, yet sometimes we act as if the baptistery represents the end of our spiritual journey rather than the beginning of a new phase.

Quality of life describes the Adventist lifestyle in the end time. How do people who live in anticipation of Christ's soon return live their lives? How do they make their choices, and how do they arrange their priorities? What is particularly "Adventist" about our lifestyle? How do our beliefs find practical expression in our lives, and how we relate to the broader public?

And then there is *unity*—a value that precedes both growth and quality of life because without it, the church as we know it and as God intended it would cease to be.

Scattering the flock

A local congregation that is fractured is not only ineffective in mission, but it is also in denial. The counsel of the Lord's servant is clear: "In union there is strength. In discord and disunion there is only weakness. . . . God wants his people to counsel together, to be a united church, in Christ a perfect whole."[2]

Throughout our history, there have always been individuals and groups that claim to want "reform," but their approach tends to be vocal, aggressively critical, and relentlessly negative. Their preferred accusations are generally "apostasy" and "abandoning historic Adventism." A number of these groups publish their own journals and establish schools and communities—all in the interests of producing a better and purer church. They quote selectively from Ellen White's writings to justify their actions, overlooking her repeated warnings against conversation that's "poisoned with criticism of the Lord's workers."[3]

Mrs. White counseled, "When anyone is drawing apart from the organized body of God's commandment-keeping people, when he begins to weigh the church in his human scales and begins to pronounce judgment against them, then you may know that God is not leading him. He is on the wrong track."[4]

If you want to find something to criticize, either in administrative leadership or local church leadership, you won't have to look very far. Elected leaders are human and sometimes just get it wrong. But destructive criticism that feeds on its own bitterness does nothing to help bring about changes that may be needed.

Some critical or offshoot groups develop around a strongly held view of end-time events (eschatology). Even though predicting the future is notoriously difficult, there's no shortage of people who put forward authoritative-sounding timelines and descriptions of what is to come. Somehow they've allowed themselves to drift toward extreme sectarian and cultish behavior, and they begin to interpret every aspect of their faith and lives through lenses of their own self-validating views of prophecy and last-day events.

Those who operate on the fringes of the church tend to bring a spirit that fractures and divides the faith community. It's a spirit of judgment, and one, I think, of spiritual arrogance. Should we ever be tempted to congratulate ourselves on our superior moral or theological position, we would do well to recall the parable of the father and the two sons (Luke 15), for it is the older son—the one who plays by the rules, the one who never disobeys—who fails to make it to the party. At times, we're too ready to presume to know the mind of God and to predict how He will deal with people at the end of the day.

Perhaps the most unhelpful line we draw within our church is the line between "conservatives" and "liberals." These labels pigeonhole people, generate suspicion and fear, and lead us to make judgments about another person's commitment or spirituality—judgments that belong only to God.

Late one Sunday night some years ago, while I was the leader of our church in Europe, I received a phone call from a man I knew well. Obviously upset, he asked me, "Why are you trying to prevent _____ [a group that conducted weekend seminars] from visiting our churches? They're just holding spiritually uplifting meetings to bring us back to historic Adventism."

Where Are We Going?

The group that this man named was an extremist fringe group, and the guest speaker at this weekend retreat was a disgruntled, separatist "critic of Israel" who claimed I was waging a campaign to stop him and others of a similar persuasion from visiting the churches of Europe.

To his credit, the man who called me that night did share with me a significant comment a friend of his made. He said that as he drove home from the retreat with several other men, they were reflecting on the "spiritual" weekend they'd had, when suddenly one of them said, "OK, if this was so spiritual, why are we all so angry at the church?"

There's something fundamentally wrong with a "spiritual retreat" that leaves us hostile toward our own church and its leaders. Critics who thrive on discrediting the church and its leaders are instruments of our enemy. Whenever and wherever they can, they tear the church down and scatter the flock. Their agenda is to provoke the very opposite of what a united church must nurture.

Unfortunately, a few elected leaders are not immune to those of this persuasion and seem comfortable in their company. Are they not nurturing this negative criticism? Where will they take us? Will they scatter the very flock they've been elected to lead?

Unity versus uniformity

We have described unity as those beliefs and values we hold in common regardless of the culture in which we live and express our obedience to Christ. Uniformity, by contrast, imposes on the church and its members a straightjacket of sameness that is alien and destructive and that places an unbearable strain on our unity. There are too many differences. We all reflect our local cultures in how we eat, dress, live, and die. We haven't all come through the same cultural conduit, and this reality affects not only our outward actions but also how we think, make decisions, and define our values. It's unrealistic, to put it mildly, for us to expect that we should all think, say, and do everything in the same way and at the same time. If we try to insist on this, we will fracture the family. A good example of this kind of issue is how we understand the role of women within the church, but there are many other issues, both large and small, that can cause us to dig in our heels and insist that "our way is the right way."

Our position statements and policies, therefore, whether in our *Church Manual* or elsewhere, must have language that acknowledges and enables cultural variations around the world. Unless a practice departs from a clear "thus saith the Lord," either in Scripture or the writings of Ellen White, the church in a local area must be allowed to be itself. It's not always easy to discern whether something should be spiritually or culturally defined, but the difficulty of the task makes it no less imperative. If we insist that our spiritual identity be expressed through a specific cultural framework, we're living in a make-believe world. And worse, if we try to impose global uniformity on our church, the unity for which Christ prayed will be taken far beyond the breaking point.

It's the responsibility of Adventist leadership to see that this doesn't happen.

Structures of unity

I've sometimes been asked whether the resources the church uses in bringing together global leadership for annual consultations is a waste of tithe money. It's a fair question, but I believe an answer can be found in our unique heritage and character as a worldwide mission movement.

Very early on in our history, we concluded that our God-given mission needed an organizational structure that's shared and integrated around the world. We've consistently rejected models of organization based on independent national churches or loose coalitions of autonomous congregations. Instead, we've said, "We place a high value on our common identity, our unique mission mandate, and our separateness from other denominations. And further, we believe that the God who raised up this movement in the mid-nineteenth century also guided us to organize as we now are."

Organizationally, this means that our structures and our processes of electing leadership are essentially the same around the world. Congregations in a local area are organized into local conferences or missions. These conferences and missions, in turn, are organized into unions, and combined they make up the thirteen world divisions of our church.

It's the unions—union conferences, union missions, and unions of churches—that are the building blocks of the General Conference.

Where Are We Going?

The presidents of these fields are all members of the General Conference's Executive Committee, which meets once a year with all its members present for what is known as the "Annual Council."

It's through the Annual Council that the international leadership considers and votes on an almost unlimited range of issues, policies, and positions that are central to the life and witness of our church. The decisions of the Annual Council become our agreed "blueprints" for how we organize ourselves, express ourselves, and pursue our mission. They're global statements, and, to that extent, they express the unity of one global Adventist Church. It's inconceivable to me that our church could speak for its global membership in this way without regularly meeting, consulting, and praying with leaders from every part of the world. And so, yes, unity does come with a price tag.

Another question that often arises about our worldwide church structure relates to money—how we arrange and use our global financial resources. While most of the tithe that's collected weekly in our churches stays within the local conference, an agreed percentage goes to support the work of the church elsewhere. Much has been written on the historical reasons and theological basis for this approach. It is part of our heritage as Adventists and an expression of who we are as a unique people with a special mission. This "financial intermarriage" connects the life of the local congregation with the global church and makes possible a worldwide reach and impact that would otherwise be utterly unattainable.

All who accept leadership functions in our church, whether at local or international levels, commit themselves to constantly consider the good of the larger church family and to do all in their power to keep the body as one.

---

1. William Barclay, *The New Daily Study Bible: Letters to the Galatians and Ephesians*, 3rd ed. (Edinburgh: St. Andrews Press, 2002), 160.

2. Ellen G. White, *The Ellen G. White 1888 Materials* (Washington, DC: Ellen G. White Estate, 1987), 903.

3. Ellen G. White, *Counsels for the Church* (Nampa, ID: Pacific Press®, 1991), 178.

4. White, *Manuscript Releases,* 1:355.

Chapter 10

A Place Where We Can Feel at Home

I would rather spend Sabbath on my own than try to carve out a place in the ice," explained one young woman who has joined the multitude of Seventh-day Adventist young people who are drifting, by slow degrees, away from the faith of their childhoods.[1] The effort needed to find a spiritual home among God's people proved too much for her.

A church building is just four walls and a roof, but what happens inside that building—the relationships that form or don't form, the acceptance we find or don't find—is absolutely critical to our spiritual journeys. Will we encounter a spirit that strengthens and equips us to be active and effective in our faith? Or will we find instead a spirit of criticism and judgment or, perhaps, just apathy, a disinterest among members to opening their circles of friendship to embrace newcomers looking for spiritual homes.

For Adventist leaders, caring for the "thermostat" of their churches is perhaps one of the most important, and difficult, assignments they will ever carry. This issue has far more than just theoretical significance for me. Many years ago, something happened to a young person who was very close to me. He was struggling with a number of things at the time, and it was not easy for him to get up each Sabbath and go to church. He arrived at the door of the church one Sabbath morning a little late and dressed in jeans. The head elder met him there and told him, "You're not suitably dressed. Go home and change your clothes." So he went home and didn't come back. And there began his long journey into the wilderness, where he has spent a long, long time. Occasionally, he comes out of the wilderness, but this is more because of the love he has for his parents and his sense of their unquenchable love for him than because he has any interest in the church.

Was this incident the sole reason he left the church? No, but when the church told him, "You really don't fit the role of someone who should be worshiping here. Go home and put on more suitable clothes"—that was a defining moment.

The church's function

As a people, we've always seen ourselves as pilgrims on a journey—"stranger[s] in a foreign country" who aren't here to stay (Hebrews 11:9). But as pilgrims headed toward the same destination, we must travel together, sit down together, commune together, and worship together in our temporary housing along the way. To Abraham, the prototype of God's pilgrims, this housing was a tent. Today, whether that "temporary housing" is a hastily built church with a dirt floor, a meeting place outdoors under trees, or an elaborate—perhaps overly elaborate—church building, the fact is that we all meet to worship in a defined physical space that we call "church." Whatever it looks like, this "temporary housing" is meant to be a safe, spiritually warm place where pilgrims can gather. It should be a place where everyone will be received with open arms and where sinners never feel out of place.

So, we must raise serious questions about our congregations. What is the dominant atmosphere of the place where we meet and worship with our fellow believers? Does our faith community reflect Ellen White's description of the church as "the theater of His grace"?[2] Or does it more closely resemble a soap opera of human nature? Does our church have the warmth of a family kitchen, or does it feel more like a clinic or laboratory?

Jesus told a story, recorded in Matthew 13:24–30, that is like so many of the parables He told; apparently simple, yet one that becomes more troubling the more you think about it. This story Jesus told deals with some critical issues about life inside the community of faith, so it's important that we understand what He's trying to teach us.

A Place Where We Can Feel at Home

The background to the story can probably be found in Jesus' teaching about the kingdom of God, an idea He presents as both a future reality—His second coming—and a present reality in the sense that Christ's followers are already considered to be citizens of His kingdom. And here we meet the problem. The people who gathered around Jesus as He traveled back and forth through Palestine were a motley group. Clearly, there were those among them whose lives had changed dramatically. But then there were also "others"—the sinners, tax collectors, and other morally dubious characters. So questions arose, What are they doing here? Are they also citizens of the kingdom? Against this backdrop, Jesus tells His story.

The scene is a wheat field approaching harvesttime. The field represents the church, the community of believers. In Jesus' story, the inevitable weeds ("tares") have grown, complicating matters and prompting a number of questions. Who is responsible for them? What should we do about them? The owner of the field isn't to blame for the weeds. They're just there. They just happen. That's the way life is.

So, what should we do about this situation? Wouldn't it be a good idea to check each plant carefully and pull out the weeds we find?

To that suggestion Jesus says an emphatic No, it's not a good idea. He doesn't even encourage us to investigate the situation. He simply says, "Leave the field alone and don't worry about it. I'll take care of it Myself in My own time."

The wheat and the weeds represent the mixed humanity that makes up our communities. Those who are of the world and those who are of Christ grow up next to each, each rooted in the same soil. Jesus' reaction to the presence of the weeds challenges our natural human inclination to fix the situation, to do whatever needs to be done to get rid of the tares that may choke life out of healthy plants. The Lord of the harvest says, "No, not now."

The story says much about how Jesus sees humanity and also about the realities of life within our church today. I believe Jesus is saying that our church is made up of a very mixed lot, and it will continue to be this way until He returns.

Yes, I believe that through the presence and power of the Spirit, the church can become a better, holier community. We can grow in commitment and devotion to our Lord, we can become more useful to Him, and we can learn from our past mistakes. But this is no reason for us to embark on a pre-Advent purging of the church, driven by a "let's toss out anything that looks like a weed" mentality. Uprooting the tares is a dangerous task best left to the Spirit. Let's never forget that this side of heaven, goodness and badness, saints and sinners, victory and defeat, wheat and tares, will remain close neighbors.

I'm not questioning the presence of people within our church who are strangers to the Lord. They may at one time have known Him, but for one reason or another they've become weary—yet they find it more convenient to stay, or staying offers more security. Possibly there's a job at stake, major family issues are involved, or maybe attending church has simply become a habit. To these sad realities the Lord says, "Leave them be for now. I'll take care of them in my own time."

Don't misunderstand me. I believe there's a difference between what the Lord is trying to teach us in this story and the flagrant abuse of the church's identity, values, standards, and mission by someone who ostensibly claims to belong to the church, but who proves himself or herself to be hostile and destructive to the church. Such a person doesn't belong, which is usually self-evident, and the church has the right to say so and take action. We call the process "church discipline." It's a tragic course of action, but one that Scripture tells us is sometimes necessary.

What we're talking about in this chapter, though, is a very different thing. It's a type of day-to-day spiritual high-handedness; an arrogant, judgmental attitude that can lead to personal ostracism and can destroy community, derail mission, and cripple the body of Christ.

Knowing the risks

As Adventist leaders, no matter what our areas of responsibility, we'll almost certainly have the experience of being presented with evidence of "weeds," accompanied by the inevitable question, "Well, what do you plan to do about it?" Before we begin weeding too vigorously in the garden, let's consider some of the reasons why weeding can be a high-risk business.

A Place Where We Can Feel at Home

The risk we take when we weed God's garden is too high because of our own humanity. As perceptive as each of us would like to think we are, the truth is that we cannot always tell the wheat and weeds apart. Do we really know fully and accurately what goes on inside another person? Are we prepared to bear the responsibility if we should happen to make a terrible mistake? When a person in our church becomes difficult—particularly if that person happens to be a teenager—could his or her behavior be the result of God's prodding, His touching that person's life? Only God knows how much latitude He will extend. I don't.

When I was in junior college in Denmark, two of my friends seemed to be constantly fighting God, themselves, and each other. For some reason, the tension in their lives seemed to undergo a buildup during a Week of Prayer on campus. As the Spirit began to touch the hearts of many students, these two boys responded to the atmosphere on campus by spearheading a vicious fistfight in the dormitory hallway. There were bloody noses and loose teeth, and the dorm dean had to separate the two boys. After considering the incident, the leaders of the school erred on the side of compassion and decided not to expel them. In the years that have followed, those two boys traveled a turbulent road with God, but I've always remembered with admiration the patient forbearance of the school administrators. God is amazingly patient, and we must learn to be patient as well—even if there's a reasonable chance the final outcome won't be what we hope.

Weeding God's garden is too risky because today is still the day of salvation. We may be able to identify and label the tares, but we mustn't forget that God hasn't finished His work.

We have so many young people who simply disappear from the church because somehow we make them feel unworthy and unwelcome. Many of them, without any help from us, already judge their spiritual self-worth too severely, and then someone from the church comes along and says, "God doesn't like you very much. He doesn't like what you wear, what you listen to, or the opinions you express."

In trying to second-guess God's mind, do we sometimes forget He may be more generous than we are? Listen to the words of the Inspired messenger: "Although in our churches, that claim to believe advanced truth, there are those who are faulty and erring, as tares among the wheat, God is long-suffering and patient. . . . He does not destroy those who are long in learning the lesson He would teach them. . . . There is to be no spasmodic, zealous, hasty action taken by church members in cutting off those they may think defective in character."[3]

When we probe, even delicately, into the spiritual lives and opinions of other people, we can cause immense harm to the church. The close spiritual bonds between us mean that our lives are closely intertwined and damage quickly spreads. In an incredibly short time, the atmosphere in our church becomes such that anyone can start to feel insecure.

Weeding in God's garden is too risky because we ourselves are harmed. When we actively nurture negativity and suspicion, something happens to us. Our misguided mission alters our characters and personalities. It's a dynamic that's readily on display in churches that have been overtaken by a spirit of criticism.

I remember an exchange between one of my former teachers and a person who was rather self-congratulatory about his own spiritual accomplishments, while being critical of those of others. My teacher said, "All right, so you're perfect, but do you have to be hostile about it?"

Breathing the air of freedom

What kind of spiritual climate are we creating in our churches? If our local churches aren't the most appealing and attractive spiritual fellowships in our communities, what are we going to do to change that? This is a leadership question.

For unbelievers, our churches are meant to be places of healing and renewal, where they'll be drawn in and find caring human relationships and spiritual help.

For believers, our churches are meant to be places to feel free, safe, and at home. They're meant to be cities of refuge, not battlefields.

I'm troubled when I worship in a church that seems to have the air of an exclusive club, a place for those who are good enough or worthy enough. Let's never forget that God is in the business of justifying *sinners,* so the church is their rightful home. The quality of the welcome we extend to sinners is more important than the quality of our church buildings or the quality of their members.

A Place Where We Can Feel at Home

I'd hate to spend my time surrounded only by people who think they have everything worked out just right. They become arrogant, clinical, and judgmental of those who still have a lot of growing to do. Their acceptance of others is always conditional. But Christ accepted us all "while we were still sinners" (Romans 5:8). Again, the words of a former teacher come back to me. He said, "Acceptance is the breath of humanity. Where acceptance is denied, breathing falters."

As Adventist leaders, we'll encounter situations when it seems difficult, if not impossible, to see the line between those things within the church that we need to confront and act upon and those things we must leave for the Lord to deal with in His own way and His own time. Whether we're pastors, lay leaders, or administrators, we love the Lord, we love our church, and we love the truth, and it's natural for us to be protective of what we love. But let's temper our protectiveness with a spirit of humility, and acknowledge that we may not always get it right.

By talking when we should be silent, I believe we can sometimes get in the way of the Spirit, who may at that very moment be speaking to the person we think is the problem, working on that person's heart, and giving him or her the opportunity to become something more. It takes restraint and self-discipline to respect the freedom of others within God's family, but those are qualities we must try to exercise.

Remember another of Christ's parables, the one recorded in Luke 13:6–8, about a man who had a fig tree growing in his vineyard. One day he came looking for fruit but found there was none, so he said to his gardener, "For three years now I've been coming to look for fruit only to find the tree barren. Cut it down! Why should I tolerate it wasting space?"

But the gardener asked for more time. He said, "Sir, leave it for one more year. I'll dig around it, fertilize it, and care for it. Maybe next year it will bear fruit. If it doesn't, well, fair enough, we can dig it up and deal with it then."

It's within our reach as local elders, pastors, and elected leaders to help create and shape the spiritual environment of our communities. My appeal is that we don't walk away from this assignment. Let's do everything we can to create a warm family spirit in our congregations.

Make them good homes where people can communicate with each other, understand and support each other, and respect each other's space. And above all, let's acknowledge that the Lord is always working to make something better out of that which, from our perspective, may be very flawed.

1. Quoted in Roger Dudley, *Why Our Teenagers Leave the Church* (Hagerstown, MD: Review and Herald®, 2000), 61.

2. Ellen G. White, *The Acts of the Apostles* (Mountain View, CA: Pacific Press®, 1911), 12.

3. White, *Testimonies to Ministers and Gospel Workers*, 45, 46.

Chapter 11

Living in Tension

Down through the centuries revival and reformation have played important roles in the spiritual lives of individuals, local congregations, and whole denominations. When we talk about revival and reformation, we're saying, or at least hinting, that we haven't yet "got it right." The words are an unmistakable call to action. We like their sound—they're so appropriate for a community concerned about spiritual matters. But there are questions we must ask if we want to experience the real thing.

Just what do these words mean for us, a community living in anticipation of the Lord's second coming? Yes, revival refers to spiritual renewal, but do we mean anything more? Revival presupposes that something has died, so we must ask, "What has died and must be brought back to life?"

And reformation—what is it that we'd like to reform? Yes, we want our spiritual lives to be as strong and vibrant as possible. This is a given for every Christian. But is it only our spiritual lives that we're trying to reform? Just what are we pursuing? When it comes to broad, all-embracing church initiatives, it's vitally important for leadership to carry the people with them in a way that engages their understanding.

As Adventist leaders, we sometimes choose language that reflects a spiritual ideal. Revival and reformation? It just feels right. We're projecting into our language our desire to move away from the daily reality toward something that's higher and better. We're describing the spiritual peak we aspire to climb but which, alas, seems elusive and out of reach. We're "down here" but wish that we were "up there." These words somehow capture the tension between what we yearn for and the reality with which we must live.

It becomes more complicated, though, when we try to spell out precisely and practically what we're talking about. So often we choose words without doing all we can to ensure that our intended meaning will be understood.

Does this matter? If we like the sound of the words we've chosen, surely they must have value. Surely we've captured something important for God's people to rally around. Is it even necessary to dig farther beneath that which sounds so self-evidently good?

Or perhaps each of us should simply bring our own private meaning to the words and interpret them in the light of our own personal experiences. But I suspect this would be a sure route to even greater confusion, for our individual experiences are not self-validating. A voice from outside must tell us whether it is good and safe to follow the trail we're on.

It's strange but true that those who want more details and more precise definitions are sometimes viewed as doubters or cynics—people who stand as obstacles in the way of spiritual renewal. I'm reminded of a fellow missionary in Nigeria whose response to a student who asked a probing question during Bible class was, "Jesus would be very unhappy if He heard you ask that question."

We tend not to like those who ask difficult questions. Those questions make us uncomfortable, so we blame our sense of uneasiness on the questioners, whom we portray as guilty because they were the ones who raised the discomforting questions. We reason, "If it isn't as clear to you as it is to me, something is wrong with *you*."

But Adventists must ask probing questions precisely because we're serious about ourselves and our lives of faith and obedience. Questions lead to dialogue, which in turn contributes to the bonding between God's people. And questions keep us alert. As an Adventist leader, don't be afraid of questions. Instead, fear silence, for apathy is far more hazardous to the body of Christ than is critical thinking.

So, let's ask the question, What do we have in mind when we talk about revival and reformation?

The ideal versus reality

Whether we call it *renewal, revival, reformation,* or *restoration,* each of us longs for something better, something more. We have personal longings and hopes for our church, and we live in constant anticipation of Christ's second coming—the moment when our deepest longings will be fulfilled. In the heart of every Adventist is an intense restlessness and dissatisfaction with the status quo. We *want* Him to return. We *pray* for Him to return. And we hope that we don't have to wait much longer.

But until His return, this is where we live—in the messy, sinful, secular reality of this world. For good and for bad, this is the landscape of our lives, where defeats and victories are our daily experiences. We're approaching the end of our journey, but for now we're still travelers.

Living in the gap between present and future, reality and ideal, is not easy. We feel the pull of both worlds. We each experience the dilemma described by the apostle Paul: "What I want to do I do not do, and what I hate I do" (Romans 7:15). Living in tension is just part of our reality, and, because of this, both victory *and* defeat will be our companions until we reach the end of our journey.

Will revival and reformation—or anything else—provide a spiritual antidote to this tension? No, I suspect not. The tension we experience will always be a part of our journey. But recognizing this tension and grappling with the challenges it presents to us may lead us to a clearer focus, to a more sustainable balance in life, and, we hope, to more spiritual victories. Before we pursue the values of renewal, let's take a look at what it means to live in tension between two worlds.

Caught between the past and the future

In Titus 2:11–14, Paul describes the two pillars on which our destiny rests—the first and second advents of Jesus Christ. Basically, Paul says, "If you want to live fully and successfully in anticipation of Christ's second coming, then you must keep your eyes fixed on His first coming." Paul sets out clearly the moral effect produced when Jesus Christ stepped into the world of humanity. His life, death, and resurrection teach us about good and bad and compel us to say Yes or No to a variety of options we have to face every day.

Notice the words Paul uses; we should be "self-controlled," do "what is good," and say "No" to "ungodliness and worldly passions." His point is that the life, death, and resurrection of Jesus Christ motivates, purifies, and empowers us for our journey. We become a pilgrim people "eager to do what is good."

It's impossible to overstate the power that flows from Christ's first coming—the few years He spent with the apostles and then the cross and His resurrection. What happened that final Passover weekend gives reality to everything that is still to come. As uncertain as we may be about the future, the ultimate outcome is not in doubt. Christ's death on the cross won the battle over evil for all eternity. His resurrection guarantees ours (see 1 Corinthians 15).

So what does it mean for us now, in our day-to-day struggles with the tension of living between two worlds?

Christ's death and resurrection give us both the motivation and the power to live our lives in preparation for His second coming. We just have to keep both events in focus. It's with that in mind that Paul wrote, "I want [you] to know Christ and the power of his resurrection" (Philippians 3:10). Commenting on this, Ellen White said, "This same resurrection power is that which gives life to the soul 'dead in trespasses and sins.' Ephesians 2:1. That Spirit of life in Christ Jesus, 'the power of His resurrection,' sets men 'free. . . .' The dominion of evil is broken."[1]

The journey isn't over. We're still pilgrims. But in Christ's first coming we find the moral power we need to stay the course.

The remaining question

So, here we stand—looking back at the Cross and the Resurrection and sensing the power that comes from those events, and at the same time gazing into the future with longing and anticipation of Christ's second coming.

We draw power from the past, and we're secure in our future, but what of our present? That's the big question now. It's a question that embraces all that we are and do as Christ's followers. It's a question that shapes all that we call "mission." The question is, What does God expect of us *today*—as individuals and as a community of believers? It's only when we're clear about the answer to *this* question that revival and reformation become something more than words in a slogan.

So, what *does* God expect of us today?

I believe He actually holds two sets of expectations for us: (1) personal, our relationship with Him and with others in His family; and (2) public, our relationships with and responsibilities to the larger world.

God's expectations for our personal lives. There is no doubt that whether you look at the Old Testament ("Stop doing wrong, learn to do right"; see Isaiah 1:16) or the New ("Hate what is evil; cling to what is good"; Romans 12:9), God's message to His people individually and collectively is, Clean up your lives. The day of the Lord will come like a thief in the night, we're told, so it's imperative that we consider "what kind of people ought you to be" (2 Peter 3:11). Living in anticipation of the Lord's coming is meant to have personal, life-changing consequences.

Paul told Titus to fix his eyes on the Cross and at the same time on Christ's return. He said he shouldn't drop either. When people maintain that perspective, they'll find the motive and the strength to say No to worldly passions.

Those last two words compose an interesting expression. What's Paul writing about?

I suspect he's writing about the habits and values that we're not very proud of and would rather not reveal. It's the work of Christ to cleanse us and help us to control them.

In this world, there are also many "innocent" things that won't be traveling with us into the next world—money and other material possessions, for example. We have to be clear about our relationships to these things. The tension is there. What do I take with me, and what will I leave behind? What about my attachment to things?

God says to His people, "I have called you out of darkness into this wonderful light. You are Mine. And because you are Mine, you are holy. Now, this is what I want you to do."

It's important that we understand clearly that we obtain our statuses as His children and as citizens of the world to come *before* our behaviors are changed and cleaned up. When we know who we are, we step out and act accordingly. It is then that holiness will display itself in a range of moral and ethical behaviors.

God also spells out clearly His expectations for the community of believers: "Live in harmony with one another, be sympathetic, love as brothers" (1 Peter 3:8, ISV). Ephesians 4:25–32 provides a good summary. It says we're to put off falsehood and speak truthfully. We're to watch our language. We're to get rid of bitterness, anger, brawling, slander, and malice. And we're to try to be nice to each other; be kind and compassionate; and forgive each other, for we have been forgiven much.

Ellen White wrote, "The truly converted man has no inclination to think or talk of the faults of others. His lips are sanctified, and as God's witness he testifies that the grace of Christ has transformed his heart. . . . Those only will enter heaven who have overcome the temptation to think and speak evil."[2]

God's expectations for our public witness. God is in the business of saving people—any and all people. He created human beings, and He intended them to be with Him forever. Now He is doing His utmost to make that happen, and Jesus Christ is the key to His mission. That, in three sentences, is what it's all about.

Where do we come in? "Christ Jesus came into the world to save sinners" (1 Timothy 1:15). That's something the world needs to know—and we're the ones to tell them.

After His resurrection, Jesus Christ gave a very straightforward vocation to each of His followers, the members of His church: "You will be my witnesses . . . to the ends of the earth" (Acts 1:8). The community of believers is God's preferred instrument to accomplish His mission, which is the salvation of humankind. This theme permeates all of Scripture.

At a private supper Jesus had with the disciples shortly after His resurrection, He said to them, "You are to be My witnesses, and I will send you power that will enable you to testify about Me. So, I'm not just telling you what you must do; I will also see to it that you can do it [see Luke 24:48, 49; Matthew 28:16–20]. Tell them who I am and what I have done. Teach them to obey everything I have taught you. Make disciples of them."

That is our all-encompassing, overriding assignment. The church has no other mission. Or as Ellen White put it, "Christ is the fountain; the church is the channel of communication."[3] And again, "The church is God's appointed agency for the salvation of mankind. It was organized for service, and its mission is to carry the gospel to the world."[4]

This is an assignment that we can't carry out at arm's length. We can't orchestrate it from the safety of our church buildings. To fulfill this assignment, the church—collectively and as individual members—must engage in the life that surrounds us.

Is there a lot of sin "out there"? Of course. But there's no way we can communicate salvation in Jesus Christ and everything that says about this life and the life to come without involving ourselves with lost people and their institutions. And so, again, we face the tension of living trapped between the ideal and the real, between the future and the present.

How far does Christ's mission reach? John tells us "the reason the Son of God appeared was to destroy the devil's work" (1 John 3:8). To me, destroying "the devil's work" speaks of a mission that goes beyond only preaching the Word, as absolutely fundamental as that is. There are also issues of health and healing, freedom of religion and conscience, education, advocacy, and being a voice for the poor and a voice against injustices and exploitation. All of these must be on the mission agenda of the church.

Christ is the Healer, the Peacemaker, and the One who sets us free. Our mission, then, is to heal, to promote peace, and to proclaim freedom. People will see God more clearly when they understand that He cares about the lives they live now, that He suffers along with them, and that He longs to take their pain and give them lives of hope.

That is our mission, but discharging it involves dealing with tension. How far can I go into the world before it taints me? Will others misunderstand what I'm doing? Will I become the subject of gossip? Can I keep my heart pure while dealing with the unclean?

When we look at how Jesus Christ lived and worked during His three-and-a-half-year ministry, we see Him among the poor, the outcasts, the lepers—the untouchables of His era. He offered healing in the here and now as well as hope for tomorrow. He offered the experience of love to those whose lives were scarred by misfortune. And Christ's message to His followers is unmistakable: "Whatever you did for one of the least of these brothers and sisters of mine, you did for me" (Matthew 25:40). That, in summary, defines the role of Christ's followers.

Which brings us back to the matter of revival and reformation. How do they relate to our fulfilling the mission Christ has assigned to us?

Revival as a goal

There is no question that spiritual renewal is critically important to our ability to stay the course. Renewal is an ongoing process, not an event and not a point we can reach and then pass. It's like the air we breathe: we can't survive spiritually without the life-giving breath that comes from God—that comes through His Word, through meditation and prayer. We won't one day reach a point on our journey when we've arrived, when we no longer need the spiritual oxygen that comes only from God.

Remember the story our Lord told about the branches and the vine? Severed from the Vine, we can do nothing and will die spiritually. Connected, we flourish and bear fruit. This describes perfectly the role of spiritual renewal in the life of Christ's followers.

Being faithful to our God-given mission is our goal. All of our energies and resources should be focused on that. This is definable and measurable. We must not allow anything to distract us. It's to fulfill this mission that we exist as a people. Engagement in it is an expression of our obedience to God, and I cannot imagine anything that, ultimately, is of greater importance than obedience to God.

May I suggest, then, that it's better to think of revival as a by-product rather than a goal? It's the natural outcome of a life of obedience.

When the church is focused on mission and assembles all of its resources to achieve more in mission, it is open to the infilling and empowering of the Holy Spirit, without which we are helpless to fulfill our assignments. And the same holds true for each of us as individuals, if we're prepared to open up our minds and hearts to the power of the Spirit.

Effective revival, then, calls for day-to-day faithfulness, a steady willingness to grapple with the tensions of living in this world while yearning for the next, being connected to the Vine while constantly reaching out with our talents and resources to accomplish our God-given mission.

The term *reformation* is perhaps in even greater need of clarification than is *revival*. *Reformation* suggests the need for specific actions, but they must also be spelled out. Reformation of what? Our fundamental beliefs? Our educational system? Our health message and dietary habits? The role of women in ministry? Supportive people cry out, "If it's good, I want it too! Help me to understand."

Our church has experienced a number of reform movements—most of whose members have viewed the church as being in apostasy and have blamed the elected leaders for taking us there. Such "reforms" thrive on negativity and criticism. Let's not nurture that approach. Is the church perfect and pure? Of course not. We have much to learn and much we should do better, for, clearly, we are still a product in the making. Remember, though, the words of inspiration: "Enfeebled and defective as it may appear, the church is the one object upon which God bestows in a special sense His supreme regard."[5]

Living in tension is our lot as long as the journey lasts, but this reality is not something for us to fear. We don't navigate the road alone. We find strength and purpose in the daily renewal that our Companion, the Comforter, is eager to give.

1. White, *The Desire of Ages,* 209, 210.
2. Ellen G. White, *Sons and Daughters of God* (Washington, DC: Review and Herald®, 1955), 348.
3. White, *The Acts of the Apostles,* 122.
4. Ibid., 9.
5. Ibid., 12.

Chapter 12

Reflections on What Lies Ahead

The LORD foils the plans of the nations;
   he thwarts the purposes of the peoples.
But the plans of the LORD stand firm forever. . . .

From heaven the LORD looks down
     and sees all mankind; . . .
  he watches
     all who live on earth (Psalm 33:10, 13, 14).

With these few words, the psalmist describes a God who is never off duty. He is present, and He cares. He wants His children to know that as they travel into an uncertain future, they will never be outside His vision.

Why is this so important? It's important because we're on a journey away from here, from our home. We're passing through time and history into the unknown. I use the word *unknown* advisedly, for the future exists in the realm of faith. Our understanding of it is shaped by the promises and imagery of Scripture, but we still see what's ahead only "through a glass darkly." We must trust the future to God, whose plans "stand firm forever."

Regardless of our particular leadership function, whether in local church ministry or elsewhere, it's important that we sometimes step back from the everyday things that absorb our attention and consider the grand sweep of the journey we're on together. We don't know how far we have yet to travel, but we do know we're on the move through enemy territory toward a sure destination. There are obstacles, and there may be hostility. "But don't be too concerned," says the Lord. "I wasn't liked much at times either." (See John 15:18, 19.) As He looks at His pilgrimaging followers, He says, "I have chosen you out of the world, so just stay the course, keep focused on Me, and I'll take you safely to the journey's end" (see verse 19).

Staying focused

As pilgrims, we're traveling over ground that's uneven and unpredictable, and we can easily be thrown off balance by the pull of competing forces that all Christians experience. We're in the world, yet separate. We yearn for the ideal, but we're living with reality. We're surrounded by things that are unattractive, disappointing, foul-smelling, threatening, unsettling, destructive, and plain evil. Yet we can't simply turn our backs on all this and walk away. Why? Because of the mission God has given us. He says, "Keep your hearts clean, but get your hands dirty." As followers of Christ the Healer, we can't turn away from everything that's ugly in the world. We must face it squarely and offer people healing and restoration both in the present and for eternity.

The terrain we're traveling over is also increasingly unstable. As I write these words, the Middle East and North Africa are wracked with political turmoil and violence, and not that long ago there were terrible upheavals in the Balkans, Asia, and many countries of Africa. No matter what direction we look, the words of our Lord seem to ring in our ears: "You will hear of wars and rumors of wars. . . . Nation will rise against nation. . . . There will be famines and earthquakes. . . . Because of the increase of wickedness, the love of most will grow cold" (Matthew 24:6–12). We say to ourselves, "This is it! It's happening! I saw it on CNN last night." But even these signs of the times can become dangerous distractions if, because of them, we turn our focus toward trying to anticipate the time and manner of our journey's end.

Our terrain may be difficult, and we may not like much of what we see around us, but this is where we are. Until we finally reach our destination, we have two equally important tasks: we must *care for mission*

119

and we must also *attend to our own personal spiritual readiness.* These are things we do simultaneously—they can't be separated. Each one strengthens and feeds the other. Through living a life of obedience, we provide the context for our own revival and spiritual renewal.

Abraham, the proto-pilgrim, illustrates the mind-set every pilgrim must have. Hebrews 11 records that by faith Abraham obeyed and left his home and country. By faith he chose to live as a stranger. By faith he looked forward to the city "whose architect and builder is God." By faith he became the father of a people. By faith he offered a sacrifice.

Faith always expresses itself in obedience. True revival and reformation will come if we will simply walk into the future, obedient to God and focused on mission.

Our fellow travelers

We're not alone on our journey—we're part of a community of travelers who are all headed in the same direction. Will we make the journey more difficult for our companions, or will we support and care for each other and make the journey easier for everyone?

Discouragement is the constant enemy of leaders. We may face it in our own walks, and we'll inevitably confront it within the community of faith, where it usually arrives in the company of criticism, negativity, and faultfinding. So, let's not sow discouragement in the hearts of any of our fellow travelers. Yes, there's plenty to pick on in ourselves and in others. Mistakes and failings aren't difficult to find, although we naturally find it easier to see them in *other* people than in ourselves. But hovering over shortcomings, our own or someone else's, can be very disheartening—a fact that the devil doesn't hesitate to use to his advantage.

God's messenger clearly warns us:

> You will often meet with souls that are under the stress of temptation. You know not how severely Satan may be wrestling with them. Beware lest you discourage such souls and thus give the tempter an advantage. Whenever you see or hear something that needs to be corrected, seek the Lord for wisdom and grace, that in trying to be faithful you may not be severe.

It is always humiliating to have one's errors pointed out. Do not make the experience more bitter by needless censure. Unkind criticism brings discouragement, making life sunless and unhappy.

My brethren, prevail by love rather than by severity. When one at fault becomes conscious of his error, be careful not to destroy his self-respect. Do not seek to bruise and wound, but rather to bind up and heal.[1]

Our words matter

One of the most potent "bandages" leaders can use to "bind up and heal" is their vocabulary. Rhetoric has power. The words we select, the labels we choose, and the tone we employ can create an environment either of support or of suspicion. We can build a culture of inclusion or exclusion. We can invite people to point fingers of blame at each other or to reach out with arms of love to embrace each other.

In chapter 5, I said that we must oppose anything that instills hatred or inflames violence in the church. Violence is always repugnant to our Lord, and that's particularly true of violence among believers.

I was in the city of Skopje, Macedonia, in the early 1990s, when the old Yugoslavia was breaking up and violent sentiments against the ethnic Serbs ruled the day. The anger and hatred ran especially strong in Skopje.

Our church in that city was rather small, and many of the members were Serbs. I was there as division president to help them elect leadership for our church in Macedonia. Normally, this was a task for the union president, but he was a Serb who lived in Belgrade, and at this time, when violence had replaced civility, his presence wasn't an option.

There were a handful of violent men among our membership in Skopje who wanted to take physical control of the central church building, and I had been warned that they might interrupt the church services that weekend. And that's exactly what happened. While I was in the pulpit Friday evening, a man jumped to his feet, shouted abuse, and demanded that my translator sit down. One of the women in the church stood up and told him to sit down and stop disturbing the spiritual hour. He ran up to her, pushed her down, grabbed her hair, and dragged her along the floor, all the while continuing to shout out a stream of verbal abuse. Of course, his actions broke up the worship service.

In all the years of my ministry, this experience was unique. That something like this could happen in an Adventist congregation was frightening as well as repulsive. How could it be?

More recently, I read of another incident of violence that took place within an Adventist setting. During a question-and-answer session after a meeting at which General Conference president Ted Wilson spoke, someone took exception to the presence, and possibly the questions, of a reporter from *Spectrum* magazine. This man expressed his frustration by punching the *Spectrum* reporter in the face. Clearly, Elder Wilson can't be held responsible for this. I know well how deeply this incident must have troubled him.

Later, I was interested to read online some comments by the man who was punched. He wrote,

> I feel as though there are things that our leaders . . . can do to . . . prevent further incidents like this one.
>
> First, our leaders can denounce . . . acts of physical violence or rhetorical aggression. . . .
>
> Second, our leaders can set the tone by refraining from employing polarizing rhetoric—the kind of language that sets "us" against "them" . . . the kind of language that creates fear and suspicion of certain groups. . . . I feel as though we must put an end to the divisive "us" vs. "them" rhetoric we use.
>
> I respectfully call on our leaders from lay members to the top church administration to set a tone of civility, peacemaking and Christian charity.[2]

Some words are just not helpful for our community of pilgrims. Labels such as "liberal" and "conservative," "rebel" and "loyalist," "progressive" and "reactionary" lead to caricatures and vilification. They create a spirit and an atmosphere that should not exist in our churches.

This is not to say that such differences don't exist. They do, and we encounter them regularly. But the language of polarization will only move people who already stand some distance apart even farther away from each other.

I suspect that as time passes and we get closer to the end of our journey on earth, our church may be increasingly vulnerable to the language of division. Even spiritual notions can play into this—the shortness of time, our personal readiness, preserving doctrinal purity, and guarding against apostasy and general worldliness. People who may see matters differently become uneasy in each other's company. Friends begin to drift apart. Being seen in the company of certain people becomes a liability. We may even begin to suspect each other's integrity or judge each other's spirituality. In an environment such as this, our journey becomes almost unbearable. Whether we serve as church elders or General Conference administrators, we must be aware of this danger and guard against it at all costs.

End-time awareness and end-time theology (eschatology) have high profiles in our church, and rightfully so. They can't be otherwise, because they are essential parts of our identity and mission. Even so, if we aren't alert, an unbalanced understanding of eschatology can inflict strange and damaging behavioral patterns on the pilgrim community. Adventist leaders have a special responsibility to guard the atmosphere within our churches jealously, and to reject language that inflames or incites. This is a matter of simple civility and charity, and it's a matter of being faithful to our Lord.

Armor for the journey

Near the end of His ministry on earth, Jesus prayed to His Father for His followers: "Protect them from the evil one" (John 17:15). Jesus knew that our journey would be hazardous. The enemies we meet along the way are nothing less than the powers of darkness, although they may well come to us in physical form. We battle against evil spiritual forces, and only the "weapons of righteousness" (2 Corinthians 6:7) will do.

The apostle Paul, writing his Epistle to the Ephesians from prison, offers some graphic descriptions of the armor each believer must have to fight off the enemy and complete the journey (Ephesians 6). It may be that Paul looked about and drew inspiration for his imagery from those who guarded him, for he presents us with a picture of a Roman soldier dressed for combat.

Before he describes this armor, though, Paul issues this counsel: "Be strong in the Lord and in his mighty power" (verse 10). The term *in the Lord* is a favorite one of Paul's, found no less than some thirty times in this epistle alone. The choice Paul presents is stark and clear: either we partner with the Lord and succeed, or we go it alone and suffer the failure of our stamina and strength. Let's not have any illusions. In the spiritual warfare we all face, no one comes away unchallenged or unscathed. We will become either conquerors or casualties.

Christ's death on the cross means that we go into this war with the Victor on our side. The universe knows it, and so does the devil. Therefore, the question is not who will win the war, but whether we will be present at the celebration of Christ's conquest. The evil one is intent on distracting as many of Christ's followers as he possibly can, turning their eyes away from the glorious victory that Christ has already won. The tragedy is that we know there will be casualties because the evil one is a master at what he does, and, in our own power, we're no match for him. But we don't face these hazards alone, for when we pledge our allegiance to Christ, He gives us the power and the protection we need to reach our destination safely.

Now, let's consider the different pieces of our armor.

The belt of truth. No doubt "truth" here refers to the truth of God's Word and the doctrines we find there, but perhaps it also embraces truth as honesty, integrity, and transparency. As pilgrims, it's not enough for us to know the text and quote the Word. Our conduct of life must match our confession.

The breastplate of righteousness. This is a metaphor for being covered by the righteousness of Christ. Using a different metaphor, John says that with this "white robe" of Christ's righteousness on, we're blessed; but without it, we're "naked and . . . shamefully exposed" (Revelation 16:15). Again, the thought is probably inclusive of both imputed and imparted righteousness—both being justified by faith and living a life that reflects what God has done for us. Men and women with upright characters are respected and protected from slanderous accusations.

Reflections on What Lies Ahead

Shoes. Paul described our footwear as the "readiness that comes from the gospel of peace." It's an image that suggests someone who is both agile and sure of foot. We have to know where we stand on the issues and challenges we meet on our journey. This clearly rests on the Word of God and our personal commitment to obey His Word. Unfortunately, some pilgrims are not sure what they stand for or are not able to present from the Bible the basis for what they hold and where they stand. Many do not make the Bible part of their daily reading.

The shield of faith. Eugene Peterson's *The Message* paraphrase expresses 1 John 5:4 this way: "The conquering power that brings the world to its knees is our faith. The person who wins out over the world's ways is simply the one who believes Jesus is the Son of God."

Faith, like the righteousness of Christ, is a gift from God. But this gift doesn't become an active, dynamic power until we make the decisions to surrender our lives to Jesus Christ. At that point, faith becomes the body-sized shield described by Paul, which can protect us from the onslaughts of evil. In the words of God to Abraham, the father of the faithful and the first pilgrim, "Do not be afraid, Abraham. I am your shield" (Genesis 15:1).

What a blessing it would be if we could always predict the direction from which the "flaming arrows" will come, but we can't. Sometimes, I fear, the arrows come from within the camp of God's own people. But our faith—our complete and unqualified trust in Jesus Christ—will keep us safe.

The helmet of salvation. In another context, as Paul considers the armor needed for spiritual warfare, he admonishes us to put on "faith and love as a breastplate and the hope of salvation as a helmet" (1 Thessalonians 5:8). The head, which is the center for understanding and decision making, needs special protection. Misguided conduct on our part is public testimony of either our failure to understand something or our failure to act on what we know. With the helmet in place, we can be sure that nothing "will be able to separate us from the love of God that is in Christ Jesus our Lord" (Romans 8:39).

The sword of the Spirit. This "sword" is nothing other than the Word of God. We use it both to defend ourselves spiritually and to drive the forces of evil away. "The word of God is alive and active. Sharper than any double-edged sword" (Hebrews 4:12). Here's how Ellen White describes the Word's impact on the first church: "They grasped the imparted gift. And what followed? The sword of the Spirit, newly edged with power and bathed in the lightnings of heaven, cut its way through unbelief. Thousands were converted in a day."[3]

The Spirit doesn't bring a new message or a new gospel. Its role is just to lead us back to the Word of God and help us to understand it.

So, I commend to you the Bible. Let's read it daily, and let's reflect on what we read, for here we'll find the armor we need to complete the journey successfully.

Hope for the journey

So many people around us are traumatized by a lack of hope, because of poverty, fear, abuse, injustice, war, or disease. It's sometimes very hard to look at what's happening in our world through the lens of hope. But pilgrims are, above everything else, a people of hope. We're constantly looking toward the horizon, confident that our destination is just ahead. Our hope motivates us, sustains us, and influences how we treat the people we meet along the way.

For a Christian traveler in need of renewed hope, there's incredible strength in the words of Psalm 121. It's one of the so-called Pilgrim's Psalms, which, according to tradition, were sung in the time of David by those who were journeying to Jerusalem for the yearly festivals.

> I lift up my eyes to the mountains—
>   where does my help come from?
> My help comes from the LORD,
>   the Maker of heaven and earth. . . .
>
> He who watches over Israel
>   will neither slumber nor sleep. . . .
>
> He will watch over your life;
> the LORD will watch over your coming and going
>   both now and forevermore (verses 1, 2, 4, 7, 8).

Reflections on What Lies Ahead

Pilgrims find no attraction in the thought of returning to the land they've left behind. Yes, I suppose there are moments when the odors from the "meat pots of Egypt" tickle the nostrils, and for a few fleeting moments the memories may be sweet, but that's all. Going back has no lasting attraction for pilgrims, for it has no future. Pilgrims have already "tasted the heavenly gift, . . . the goodness of the word of God and the powers of the coming age" (Hebrews 6:4, 5), and they have a firm resolve.

Pilgrims have heavenly citizenship, and they know it. And it's not merely a hopeful promise—it's a reality (see Romans 8:16, 35–39). "Our citizenship is in heaven," so "we eagerly await a Savior from there" (Philippians 3:20).

As leaders of God's pilgrim people, may we be found faithful on that day.

---

1. White, *Testimonies for the Church,* 7:265.

2. Jared Wright, February 2, 2011, (15:24), comment on Jiggs Gallagher, "Violence at President Wilson's California Speech," *Spectrum Magazine,* retrieved March 9, 2011, from http://spectrummagazine.org/blog/2011/02/25/violence-president-wilsons-california-speech/#comments.

3. White, *The Acts of the Apostles,* 38.